Abortion, Choice, and Contemporary Fiction

Abortion, Choice, and Contemporary Fiction

The Armageddon of the Maternal Instinct

Judith Wilt

The
University
of Chicago
Press

Chicago & London

JUDITH WILT is professor of English at Boston College. Her
most recent book, *Secret Leaves: The Novels of Walter Scott,*
is also published by the University of Chicago Press.

The University of Chicago Press, Chicago 60637
The University of Chicago Press, Ltd., London
© 1990 by The University of Chicago
All rights reserved. Published 1990
Printed in the United States of America
99 98 97 96 95 94 93 92 91 90   5 4 3 2 1

LIBRARY OF CONGRESS CATALOGING-IN-PUBLICATION DATA

Wilt, Judith, 1941—
    Abortion, choice, and contemporary fiction : the armageddon of the
maternal instinct / Judith Wilt.
        p.   cm.
    Includes bibliographical references (p.   ).
    ISBN 0-226-90158-0 (alk. paper)
    1. American fiction—20th century—History and criticism.
2. Abortion in literature.   3. Birth control in literature.
4. Motherhood in literature.   5. Mother and child in literature.
6. Mothers in literature.   7. Women in literature.   8. English
fiction—20th century—History and criticism.   I. Title.
PS374.A24W55   1990
813'.509353—dc20   89-20595
                                                              CIP

"There is no general doctrine which is not capable of eating out our morality, if unchecked by the deep-seated habit of direct fellow-feeling with individual fellow-men." (and women)

Middlemarch, George Eliot (Mary Ann Evans)

This book is dedicated to all my women teachers, especially my mother, Mrs. Katherine Steffen Wilt Campbell, and Sister Mary Agnella of St. Francis Academy, the late Dr. Frances Chivers of Duquesne University, Professors Mary Burgan at Indiana University and Lynne Hanley at Hampshire College, and Dean Carol Hurd Green at Boston College.

Contents

Preface

I first began to think about abortion as literary matter in the mid-1970s, when I was assigned to teach a course in twentieth-century American literature which paired John Barth's *The End of the Road* and Joan Didion's *Play It as It Lays* as examples of post-realistic fiction. The presence of abortion at the heart of each plot seemed more than coincidence. Abortion declined to leave either the front pages of newspapers or the plots of novels after the Supreme Court decision of 1973; as I began to look, I found it everywhere.

In Providence, Rhode Island, in 1985, a husband accuses his wife of killing their four-month-old daughter, because, after four abortions, she found she couldn't parent a live child. A young man burns down a house, it is reported, because his girlfriend aborted "his" child. During the 1984–85 television season an episode on "Hill Street Blues" presented a right-to-life demonstrator with a special dilemma—his too-enthusiastically waved demonstration sign caused an information seeking, not abortion seeking, young woman to slip and miscarry. If he sticks by his argument that the fetus is a person he is guilty of manslaughter; if he lets his defense attorney plead the fetus is by Supreme Court definition not a person, he goes free. In Ed McBain's 1985 mystery, *Lightning*, a reluctant father of four rapes only Catholic right-to-life women, the same women, until they become pregnant, so that, pregnant, they will face the "choice" their religion forbids.

As I complete this work in the summer of 1988 the stories continue. Summer paperback releases include Sara Paretsky's mystery, *Bitter Medicine*, where the right-to-lifers' bombing of a free clinic that occasionally performs abortions is prominently featured and deplored; John Gregory Dunne's latest lifestyles-of-the-rich-and-famous-Catholics novel, *The Red, White and Blue,* where the only weak spot in the tough-as-nails female protagonist's makeup seems to be the reason she aborted her husband's father's child ("I won't talk about the scrape, Jack," she says, and, to the reader's bewilderment, she never does); playwright Marsha Norman's first novel, *The Fortune Teller,* where the kidnappers of twenty-two children are revenging themselves on an abortionist culture they blame for their daughter's early death by abortion; and the true-life story of Diane Downs (*Small Sacrifices,* by Ann Rule), convicted for trying to kill her three children in order to attract back her lover. According to psychiatrists Diane Downs loved to be pregnant, dreamed of a future as a continuing surrogate mother, but couldn't be a parent. And the July issue of *Soap Opera Digest* confirmed what we steady watchers knew: abortions are "out" and miscarriages are "in" this season, while pregnancy is, as ever, a staple of that group of narratives.

The confines of art are no less grotesque and complicated than the purlieus of life when it comes to abortion. But at least the truth of the author's intention and his/her achievement remains stable enough to be looked at and argued over. That is what, with humility, I propose to do in the following essays. At the same time, I feel the need to begin with history, especially case history. For lives, actual experiences, are surely the basis of art; and the fact is that the reality and multiplicity of experience are always in danger of being overwhelmed by, hyperordered by, art. I cannot really avoid this danger in a book of literary criticism, but I am aware of it, and aware, too, of a new spirit abroad, as *Roe vs. Wade* comes under increasing attack: a spirit which would delegitimize the rough and multiplex female experience that went into the abortion law reform movement in favor of the more totalizing perspectives of law or art. I want this book not to harbor that spirit.

The reader may well assume that I bring a personal attitude as well as literary ones to this task. I do. Let me see if I can express it. As a feminist and a Catholic, I believe a woman's freedom to abort a fetus is a monstrous, a tyrannous, but a *necessary* freedom in a fallen world. In an unfallen world (or in the moment of grace) there would be no necessity, therefore no freedom: the freedom is a sign of our dire necessity and coterminous with it. I have some sympathy with the principle, if not always with the methods, of those who would thrust the woe of this freedom into the arena of debate and the field of consciousness. But I must call, even for myself, and certainly for my countrywomen, for the necessary freedom of choice within which to make my soul, if I can, free from that necessity.

Introduction: The Wreck, and the Story of the Wreck

We live in a civilization," says psychoanalyst Julia Kristeva with brilliant simplicity, "where the *consecrated* (religious or secular) representation of femininity is absorbed by motherhood," a motherhood which essentially represents "the *fantasy* . . . of a lost territory."[1] This territory is plenitude, absolute fullness. The child remembers the mother as the experience of plenitude; the adult, inhabiting a limited body and personhood, desires progeny, extension, plenitude. Earlier psychoanalytic thinkers, preoccupied with Freud's vision of the female as a creature of "lack," explained the woman's desire to bear a child as a move to recapture the penis, the male power, absent from her own "castrated" body, or to actualize the core of a hidden female self. Both of these Freudian theories objectify the child as a completion of "valid" female identity: the male is born as its mother's phallus, the female as its mother's "best" self. The daughter is left, as we shall see in Toni Morrison's *Beloved*, to seek out her self again in motherhood.

Heterosexuality and maternity, inherited, enforced, ascribed—the compensations for an all-pervading "lack." Many feminist thinkers argue that this vision of heterosexuality and maternity only expresses, and works in, patriarchy. In a new world envisioned by some feminist theory, however, a new sexuality, a born-again maternity, should offer wider possibilities to the individual, possibilities for integrating lives, creating new lives. While requiring activity and community, even modes of "completion," these possibilities would not be premised on lack, nor denigrate as lacking the sex whose body was, for all of us, the first experience of plenitude.

1

Early forms of this envisioned new world focused on critiques of the world as it is. So for the most part do the fictional stories about patriarchally constructed heterosexuality, maternity, choice, and abortion or birth that I will treat in the four essays that follow this introduction. That theory and these stories often suggest, fiercely or ruefully, that heterosexual maternity can have *no* place in the envisioned non-patriarchal world. More recent feminist theory has returned to maternity, especially "pre-Oedipal" maternity, as a ground for re-imagining human relationships.[2] This theory culminates in Julia Kristeva's paradoxical distinction between heterosexuality, indeed sexuality itself, and maternity; whereas heterosexuality has arguably been entirely colonized by male dominance, maternity retains an edge of its original nature, its original wildness, not fully captured even by the huge apparatus of idealization, repression, reduction, and manipulation, which culture has applied to it.[3] Here the "realistic novel" cannot yet travel, though writers of fantasy (Ursula LeGuin, Monique Wittig) have marked out some parts of the path. Meanwhile, the very omission of "the mother" from much cultural representation, argues feminist film critic E. Ann Kaplan, provides some hope, since it shows that patriarchy is "not monolithic, not cleanly sealed."[4] Gaps appear through which women can begin to ask questions and introduce change.

The makeshift seals of culture over maternity have now been split wide for a generation over the issue called abortion in the political and medical arena. The issue is in fact maternal choice. Though some element of maternal choice has been part of the lore of women back to its traceable dawn, in this generation "the maternal" exists no longer repressed in the unconscious, or as "the natural," operating as biological or psychological "instinct." For a larger part of the planet's women than ever before, the maternal now exists on a spectrum reaching from the preconscious domain of fantasy to the hyperconscious discourses of medicine, law, psychology, economics, religion, and politics which structure choice. However rationalist these discourses strive to be, though, one hears always in them the disturbed echo of the preconscious root: "the fantasy of a lost territory."

From this angle, it seems possible that the apocalyptic terror of pro-life men and women, the subtle unease of pro-choice women and men, has some reference to this fantasy. Consciousness itself implies loss. Choice may not always result in abortion, but rhetorically it is abortion. In this respect every pregnancy precipitates a loss, not just those that end in abortion; just as every pregnancy at some level makes a mother, not just those that end in birth. What is lost, according to the pro-life position, is "the baby," fetishized projection appropriating the male other, or enacting the female self, or contacting an irrational reality, nature, or God. What is lost, admits the pro-choice position, is the choice not made, the possibility (completed maternity, or continuing independence, or limited maternity) that was set aside. What is lost, conflictless "maternal instinct," is replaced by conflict-ridden human choice. The quest is for plenitude, the seamless enactment of multiple simultaneous desires, to be *and* not to be "the mother." The abortion debate, pouring out of the gap in patriarchy's construction of "the maternal," is part of this quest.

Debate about abortion may begin with reasons, proceed to statistics, but it always comes down, really, to stories. "Your side doesn't tell the whole story." "But *your* side doesn't tell the *true* story." "This dramatic case history proves our point." "But *this* dramatic case history proves *our* point." "This tearful recantation from someone who used to believe as you do shows that our argument gets to the human heart of things." "But *this* poignant confession from someone who claimed to believe as you do shows that *our* argument answers human needs." Or, more deeply fought: "Your gender, age, experience, invalidates you as teller of this story, even if it is your own." "No, *your* religious training, or political ideology, or emotional exhaustion incapacitates *your* telling."

The abortion debate rides on overlapping narratives of pregnancy/birth. One is abstract, scientific, or religious: in it, life, transcendent, seeks its own extension, and the drama of individuals is a subplot. Two other narratives are essentially female: in one, woman gives birth to the Other—angelic, demonic, mystified; in the second, woman like all humans, only half-born at parturition, struggles toward the birth of an adult self. In this second female narrative, pregnancy/birth may offer a useful complication towards that desired resolution: "I had been trying to give birth to myself," says Adrienne Rich of her first pregnancy, "and in some grim, dim way I was determined to use even pregnancy and parturition in that process."[5] Or pregnancy/birth may be in competition with it. The college friend who found her an abortionist just in time "handed me back my life," says Alice Walker. In exchange, "that week I wrote without stopping . . . almost all the poems in *Once*."[6]

Present in all these narratives, the ones women tell themselves, the ones society tells them, and especially the ones artists tell about women, are values of choice, freedom, knowledge. Choice, it seems in these narratives, reaches toward error when it becomes the management of the human, freedom when it becomes the greed to control utterly time and space, and knowledge when it ceases to strive against, re-create if necessary, the unknown. Since the Greeks, artists have warned that human beings should leave a space in the imagination for the work of the gods, an opening in the hero's plan for the divine surprise. The artists, allied in their bones with the notion of the surprise, can do no other. From Sophocles' Creon to the characters of Margaret Atwood and John Irving, it is the would-be manager they surprise; irresistible rational force meets immovable natural object.

Abortion, a malleable topos, seems to work most often under this law of plot: if abortion represents the unholy domain of control, the plot will dissent from, perhaps thwart it. To support abortion, which lends itself so easily to the unholy domain of control, the novelist will have to place the act in the domain of surprise, resistance to control. If a man attempts to control a woman through pregnancy, the plot will resist with abortion (Marge Piercy's *Braided Lives*); if a man attempts to control a woman through abortion, or a woman attempts to control "nature" with choice, the plot will resist with pregnancy (Margaret Atwood's feminist *Surfacing*, Faulkner's emphatically nonfeminist *As I Lay Dying*).

Furthermore, no novelist can resist the insistent pressure to provide some kind of aftermath for an abortion. Even when the narrative supports the structure of choice, even when it supports the particular choice which is its subject (Gail Godwin's *A Mother and Two Daughters*, Marsha Norman's *The Fortune Teller*), the "product of conception" has its "birth" in the refusal, of character or narrator, to stop contemplating the conception. "That's all there is to it," the confident feminist daughter in *The Fortune Teller* says of the easy parameters of choice she foresees, and "That's all there is to it?" returns the meditating feminist mother, dumbfounded and unconvinced.[7] This pressure comes only partly from the novelist's moral universe; it comes most deeply from the demands of story itself.

Pregnancy, of course, is the ultimate surprise, the roof lifting just as you've finally got the doors and windows closed. Artists can make this malleable surprise play in dozens of ways, too. The narrative, or the character within the narrative, can define pregnancy as the proof of true womanhood or manhood, the reward or punishment of God, the fruit of good or bad sexuality, the sign of a relationship knitting or sundering, the extension, transformation, exposure, of the self (individual or social) which projects it. This definition will radically color the climax of the pregnancy narrative, whether it is birth or termination, and whether that narrative is a case history or a work of art.[8]

The telling of this story is a site of profound anxiety, not only for the teller (again, individual or social) whose self-definition stands thus revealed, but also for the hearer (or reader) who must encounter in this story the specter of his or her own potential not having been. If the pregnancy narrative ends before birth, even by accident but especially by choice, it leaves two ghosts in its wake: the ghost of the child that might have been and the ghost of the self that might have borne and parented that child. And, for a moment, the hearer may experience, in the confrontation with these imaginable but not real beings, the radical contingency of his or her own consoling "reality."

In the several books of case histories about pregnancy/birth or pregnancy/abortion decisions—books on all sides of the issue—women and some men testify to the presence of these ghosts in themselves. The pro-life movement defines these hauntings as the guilty price of choice made wrongly. For those who continue to confirm their choice of abortion, the ghosts remain as well, evidence of that desire for a plenteous and boundless self (one which both did and did not give birth), which the philosopher Jacques Lacan structures as the first stage of human desire. In Lacan's "imaginary" mode or order of being, the pre-Oedipal human seeks his or her mirror "image" and gladly reaches for it, believing, falsely as it turns out, that the oceanic fullness and connection it feels in its relationship with "world" will be located and confirmed there, in that image, which is itself. Alienation, limitation, boundary, comes with the inevitable human immersion in language, civilization, Lacan's "symbolic" order. Here the great power gained with one's first adventures in controlling reality by naming it barely compensates for the dismay felt at the loss of the image of self as all, or the terror felt upon the recognition that the word which enables the self to trap and hold some parts of the real is also what entraps, grounds, the self.

The narrative of pregnancy/abortion, then, with its ghostly outlines of unreachable plenitude through the looking glass of the self and its ultimate choice of the fiction of control—control of the body and its image, control of the future self in the making—takes us right back to the line we once crossed from the all-desiring imaginary to the rational symbolic, from the limitless world where choice has no meaning because no alternative excludes another, to the world we mostly think we have to live in, the world of either/or.

This has ties to what Kristin Luker's study of pro-choice and pro-life activists uncovered: that the two groups have internally consistent, mutually exclusive worldviews.[9] The pro-life worldview, like Lacan's imaginary, is immersed in, and at home with, transcendence, confident that all the "surprises" of human experience have a grace in them; that all new directions, even those that hit with the force of a blow, are one direction; that the plenteous self, the oceanic unity in the mirror, will be reached in the post-mortal end. The pro-choice worldview, bereft or uncertain of this end, dwells in Lacan's symbolic order, ready to speak, ready to plan, ready for the long, complex arc of reasoned thought toward best possible choice.

From this standpoint, paradoxically enough, the pro-life worldview, so apparently narrow and rigid in practice, so gender structured and hierarchical, prides itself on a philosophical vision of limitlessness—a vision that all possibility may be actuality; while the pro-choice worldview, so multivalent and uncoercive in practice, so committed to the relaxation and crossing of gender and other boundaries, founds itself (pride is not quite the word) on a philosophical vision of human limits—a vision of oscillating losses and gains. And "the fall," the demonic underside, of the pro-life worldview, Luker speculates, would be guilt, as its theorists and practitioners confront the difficulty of living up to the ideal of the limitless yes to creation. The shadow on the pro-choice worldview, as its theorists and practitioners confront both the difficulty of making moral choices where the guidelines have been so dissolved and the inevitable human weariness or shallowness that deserts the long arc of reasoning for the shortcuts of rationalization, would be anxiety (Luker, 186).

In a key Adrienne Rich poem the speaker, a solitary diver, seeks the truth of the "fall" of her world, and ours. "Diving into the Wreck," while not a poem explicitly about abortion or motherhood, offers a vivid metaphor, I think, for that search for the "lost territory" of the mother, motherhood, and an unseparated and "blissful" childhood, which I have argued lies beneath the abortion debate. The speaker takes, in addition to the rubber flippers and oxygen mask, which both enable and distort her, "a book of myths," which gives somewhat dim and coded directions, and a camera, for she intends in this quest to find "the wreck and not the story of the wreck / the thing itself and not the myth."[10] Encountering "the drowned face . . . whose breasts still bear the stress," the speaker becomes both male and female, becomes ultimately both speaker and listener/reader: "I am she: I am he. . . . We are, I am, you are." Portentous, locked in gaze with the sun, the wreck says nothing of itself: though the camera records "the half-destroyed instruments / that once held to a course / the water-eaten log / the fouled compass," the poem, fearful lest it become just one more page in the book of myths, leaves the multiple speaker/listener/questor storyless, staring at the thing itself, not even ready to say whether the quest was an act of "cowardice or courage."

Yet, of course, with its echoes of Icarus and Atlantis, of the Apple, the Flood, and the Crucifixion, above all with its overlay of feminist "revision" of the story of Eve, the poem cannot ultimately free itself from story, must at last make another in the dimly guiding book of myths. Indeed, its very minimalism, the "threadbare beauty" of "the ribs of the disaster" presented, renders "this scene" immediately capturable by the scenario the listener/reader brings. The thing itself glimmers, real but unreachable, like the infant's image in the mirror, awaiting the story that will embody it.

The social narrative of women's lives, the telling of true stories in public, itself has a kind of history to it, based on what was held to be necessary, interesting, or troubling about women. Much sacred storytelling from the dawn of the art reflects the narrative of (sacred) women giving birth. After the dawn, the focus of narrative moves to the crisis point of sexual and social initiation, courtship and marriage, as society charts the preparation of its women for giving birth. This sunny narrative is accompanied by (at least) three shadow narratives, stories of woman's fall, disaster, wreck, which emerge, whether in life histories or works of art, when the social arrangement meets the human female fact. One narrative, following the woman stepping (or being pushed) aside from the preferred arrangements of courtship, encompasses seduction or rape and abandonment. Culturally celebrated fictions depicting this, a *Clarissa*, a *Tess of the D'Urbervilles*, are deeply punitive of the victim even as they compassionate or ennoble her. They inevitably suggest that if she had scurried more quickly into a decent marriage she would have escaped her fate. A second narrative, directly concerned with marriage, focuses on adultery. Here again culture's fictions, a *Scarlet Letter*, an *Anna Karenina*, intend to ennoble the socially thwarted but passionately risk-taking human spirit. But the end (maybe even goal) is punishment, or worse, self-punishment.

A third narrative, buried largely in private discourse until recently, moves the focus of woman's story to maternity and follows her departure from that arrangement towards infanticide and abortion, a departure deeply entangled again with punishment, especially self-punishment. That is the narrative I wish to study here: first, briefly in the life histories caught up in, made use of by, the public discourse of abortion, and then more extensively in readings from (mostly) novels which reflect and help shape that public discourse. In all of these stories, the shape of the thing itself, the wreck as wreck, the wreck of the principle of unlimited life by the structures of patriarchal culture, or on the hard rock of human mortality, is visible. But the detail, whether the wrecked figure beneath the story-refracting water is child, woman, principle, or culture, can only be supplied by the story—and the story's story.

"Wragg Is in Custody"

S peech quails before the spectacle of women transgressing accepted codes of motherhood. One of the most poignant and infuriating examples of this quailing occurs in Matthew Arnold's influential nineteenth-century essay, "The Function of Criticism at the Present Time." Angry at the fictions of self-praise emanating from liberal Englishmen of the time, Arnold draws the reader's attention to a newspaper paragraph which contradicts the comfortable can-do spirit of the nation:

> A shocking child murder has just been committed in Nottingham. A girl named Wragg left the workhouse there on Saturday morning with her young illegitimate child. The child was soon afterwards found dead on Mapperly Hills, having been strangled. Wragg is in custody.[11]

Arnold grasps this fact of maternal infanticide as the index to what's amiss in the liberal, utilitarian England of the 1850s. He proposes that we all mutter mutinously under our breaths, "Wragg is in custody," as a talisman to break out of the spell of self-absorption and self-satisfaction coming from liberal politicians who feel they can solve any problem by a practical reform. He notes with ambiguous, personal turmoil that the newspaper format, "Wragg," dehumanizes, de-Christianizes, desexes the malefactor, who is also a victim. But, memorably shifty jump over the abyss of social analysis, what for Arnold makes Wragg such a certain and rough talisman is less her story than her sound: "Has anyone reflected what a touch of grossness in our race, what an original shortcoming in the more delicate spiritual perceptions, is shown by the natural growth amongst us of such hideous names—Higginbotham, Stiggins, Bugg!" Wragg.

Wragg's own story, harsh as her name no doubt, never reached Arnold, whose ears would likely have shuddered closed at it, like his lips. Nineteenth-century stories of antimotherhood, muttered under the breath, prepared the way for a speech that breaks out of the law's custody in the twentieth century, as male journalists and doctors, finally women themselves, begin to tell Wragg's story—the story of infanticide, abortion, female violence from what Adrienne Rich calls the victimized "heart of maternal darkness" (*Of Woman Born*, 260).

*

The twentieth-century discourse of abortion typically begins by adverting to a climate, indeed a conspiracy, of silence, which the narrative will transgress with stories, case histories. The assumption here is almost that speech itself will heal the divisions in, point a clear direction for, culture through stories that, prelegalization, complexify the law's or the church's rigid posture; stories that, postlegalization, complexify the law's or feminism's supposed airy meliorism.

Lawrence Lader's path-breaking 1966 study, *Abortion*, begins: "Abortion is the dread secret of our society . . . relegated for so long to the darkest corners of fear and mythology that an unwritten contract virtually requires that it remain untouched and undiscussed."[12] Linda Bird Francke's 1978 *The Ambivalence of Abortion* opens with the story of her 1973 abortion, which she published anonymously in 1976 in *The New York Times;* it touched off an explosion of debating letters, many detailing the writer's own first-time-told experience with abortion choice. Introducing them, Francke declares, "Abortion is not new by any means. But confronting the fact of it without furtiveness and danger is."[13] Paula Ervin's 1985 *Women Exploited*, written from the perspective of the movement called Women Exploited by Abortion (WEBA), opens with a case history that had difficulty reaching national or "centrist" publication, a woman's "They told me it wasn't a baby but now I know it was" story. Ervin seeks the hidden impact of legalized—even, as she and WEBA see it, culturally valorized—abortion on the women who chose it: "The answers have been slow in coming because, even though Adele's experience has been blessed by law, it is not a subject easily discussed."[14] Ellen Messer and Kathryn May's 1988 *Back Rooms: Voices from the Illegal Abortion Era*, prefaces its thirty-three stories with a description of the cultural amnesia among the young that paradoxically forms another kind of silence that must be broken through.[15] And, of course, the experience of men undergoing at second hand, but often with considerable pain, the traumas of abortion—their relative exclusion from the decision-making process often reveals the exclusions and isolations that already characterize the relationship—is now being studied, too.[16]

Noisy in the foreground until recently has been the story of three male professions—medicine, law, philosophy/theology—contending for the right to define and control the nature, purpose, and process of women giving birth. Even the doctors and lawyers, for instance, were surprised to find that the absolutist story many Christian theologians and philosophers had been telling about the sacredness of life from the moment of conception was a fairly recent version of the story of life. Up through medieval times a different story, based on Aristotle's philosophical/scientific theory of a three-stage fetal gestation from vegetable to animal to human "soul," had held that life and personhood, and hence sin, begins at quickening, which may occur in the fetus as long as ninety days after conception.[17] The law, which had in Greek and Roman cultures sanctioned the right of a father-controlled family to use both abortion and infanticide, which had responded similarly to population control imperatives in post–World War II Japan and Eastern Europe, was a story of oscillation, not certainty. Medicine, whose founding Hippocratic oath contains an explicit injunction against abortion, has over the centuries simultaneously evolved ingeniously safer ways both to abort and to continue the life of the fetus.[18] And it is on the desire of this profession to maintain the right it won in the nineteenth century over the birth scene against the intervention of the other two professions that the abortion discourse in the twentieth century has developed. This is the story, "the doctor's dilemma," that got told most often, most publicly, as the rethinking of nineteenth-century abortion statutes began.

During the nineteenth century, English and American common law, which had essentially rendered abortion before quickening noncriminal, began to give way to statutory laws encouraging birth.[19] The statutes often included a qualification allowing profes-

11

sional medical judgment to intervene with abortion on behalf of the life of the maternal patient—one respected profession on the rise deferring to another. Abortion as "the doctor's dilemma," to quote Lader (see chapter 5), begins as the profession consolidates itself against the "unskilled" and unlicensed purveyor of quack nostrums, the greedy amateur, and, of course, female healers and midwives. In its fight to keep control over the birth scene as a tide of puritan legislation broke over the late nineteenth- and early twentieth-century American landscape, medicine ceded decision making to the profession in the abstract. Hospital committees, rather than individual doctors, were to determine whether the one legal ground for abortion, that pregnancy would endanger the life of the mother, had been met.

As medicine all but eliminated many of the old physical complications of pregnancy and began, under the impact of psychiatry, to establish other, mental conflicts as life and health threatening, the decisions of hospital committees, as well as of individual doctors, became unpredictable. A study by two Stanford University researchers in 1959 offered a potential case history for therapeutic abortion to twenty-six California hospital boards; ten of those answering approved the case, and twelve rejected it.[20] As the lawyers for hospitals watched the doctors divide, they felt increasingly compelled to counsel their medical boards to reject all but a "strict constructionist" vision of the life of the mother condition, and so what Lader in 1967 termed the doctor's dilemma became what Luker's 1984 account called more largely the professionals' dilemma.

What the doctors and the lawyers wanted by the 1960s was a set of reformed abortion statutes which would clarify the grounds by which a "professional" decision could be made by the woman and her doctor—and his lawyer. Kristin Luker argues that the very success of the state-by-state legislative reform in the mid-sixties arose from the fact that the debate seemed enclosed in professional, almost technical, argument. The philosophical issues that underlay the professionals' dilemma—personhood, womanhood, motherhood—had barely been touched outside the rarified circles of professional forums and legislative hearings. The public at large remained relatively ignorant of how deeply divided it really was about these issues. And the two extraprofessional constituencies which would conduct the debate that still rages—those who have a moral opposition to abortion, and those who would come to hold that the right to choose whether or not to give birth is the cornerstone of the freedom, or personhood, of women—were still largely, says Luker, "unawakened" (66–67).

It was the latter constituency that wakened first, and its medium of self-awareness was stories. Dozens of separate groups which together came to be called The Women's Movement set up semiprivate and then public forums where women told the stories of lives lived at odds with the social construction of womanhood, marriage, and motherhood that the law, the doctor, the cleric thought were in force. The stories electrified into speech the women in the audiences who were full of their own withheld stories, and the magnitude of the dissent and the will to change became apparent. Diane Schulder and Florynce Kennedy's 1971 account of abortion reform in New York state begins with a March 1969 forum set up by the radical feminist Redstockings group: "Twelve young women faced an audience of more than three hundred men and women and with simplicity and calm and occasional emotion and even humor . . . rapped about their own abortions."[21] Kristin Luker's account of California reform quotes an official of the Society for Humane Abortions, founded in the mid-sixties: "We didn't sell anyone anything. We didn't have to. It was a terrible need, and all you had to do was start the conversation and people would just come from everywhere" (98).

The conversation—if you speak the story of your abortion, I'll speak mine, too—ran like wildfire through the country, Luker remarks, not because women suddenly changed their minds about the morality of past choices or future ones, but because a new climate of speech about sexuality was developing.

> For many people abortion was "unspeakable" not because
> it represented the death of a child but because it repre-
> sented "getting caught" in the consequences of sexuality.
> Sex, not abortion, was what people didn't talk about. (129)

On the other hand, as the historian of culture, Michel Foucault, has provocatively argued, it isn't as if western bourgeois culture has kept quiet about sex. Rather, we have had several centuries of "incitement to discourse": "Not only did western culture speak of sex and compel everyone to do so, it also set out to formulate the uniform truth of sex. As if it suspected sex of harboring a fundamental secret."[22] From philosophers to mass market advertisers, human beings set out to "uncover," says Foucault ironically, what they had already been noisily broadcasting in the light of day (158), that human nature and behavior, for good or ill, is fundamentally linked to (governed and manipulated by) sexuality. For Foucault, this newly created "truth" became the rationale for whole new departments in medicine, law, and theology: departments which bid to exercise control over the speaking of sexuality. The newly galvanized women's speech of the 1960s, which sought to break the tie of woman's sexuality to motherhood called natural by the reigning discourses in medicine, law, and theology, was from this perspective simply another eruption in a medium already saturated with speech about sex. It was a new speech with a revolutionary potential, indeed, but also, as many of the more astute speakers recognized quickly, with the capacity to become institutionalized in a repressive discourse. This is WEBA's charge. But on the left, Schulder and Kennedy's 1971 book on the New York reform movement includes long quotations from an early Black Panther pamphlet warning about abortion as potential "black genocide." Dissenting, the authors nevertheless note "numerous signs that oppression of women can easily be reversed into enforced limitation on reproduction. This has already been felt by the nonwhite, and the urban and rural poor" (185).

Two examples of women's speech that first saw print in 1969 show the professionals' dilemma giving way to women's stories. In that year died Dr. Robert Spencer, a physician in the small town of Ashland, Pennsylvania, who as "Dr. S" was one of the models of "the skilled abortionist" in Lader's 1967 book on abortion. A respected hometown native, friend of all the public officials, Dr. Spencer believed in humane abortion as part of family practice; he did careful, inexpensive abortions for more than forty years for thousands of grateful east coast women. Lawrence Lader reports Dr.

Spencer's dilemma: one of his first patients, a pregnant mother of eight with severe liver damage whose husband, and priest, forbade the abortion the doctor recommended, died shortly after childbirth. After that, he treated his patients as he and they thought best, regardless of the law (47).

Susan Brownmiller discussed Dr. Spencer in a 1969 *Village Voice* article: "He had gotten into abortion work during the 1920s through the supplication of the miners' wives in the Pennsylvania coal country, and his work for the miners won him. . . , some said, the protection of the United Mine Workers." The article focused on Dr. Spencer's solution to the doctor's dilemma but also contained a woman friend's story: "He had given her an assortment of pills to ward off infection and build up her strength. He seemed concerned about her, downright fatherly. He didn't make her think she had done something wrong" (portions of article reprinted in *Abortion Rap*, 68–69).

Later that year a woman published an anonymous account of her 1953 abortion at Dr. Spencer's office in *Cavalier* magazine (ambiguous venue, to be sure!). She briefly recalls a "soft-spoken but passionate diatribe" from Dr. Spencer about the need to break bad laws, followed by the signing of a paper agreeing to assume part of his court costs if he were to be prosecuted on her account. But she later learned he had abandoned that part of the ritual: "My files were getting too full" (article reprinted in *Back Rooms*, 221).

The essay concentrates, however, on the woman's own grateful experience—"What a fitting close to the only meaningful Easter of my life—it was I who had risen and I who had been given a new life" (222)—and details contrastingly grim experiences of women friends with unskilled or unscrupulous abortionists. The article climaxes by making two points (one direct, one indirect) about "responsible" abortion that will become key in much storytelling by women.

> In destroying a life (and I never deceived myself about that: I wept bitterly a few weeks later when I found in a biology book a life-size drawing of an eight-week embryo), he saved mine. He saved me from a life with a man I didn't love,

and he freed me for the life I have now with a superb husband and two magnificent daughters. (224)

We can see these two points made again in a study of the way twenty-nine women made decisions about abortion, which became part of the material Carol Gilligan used to elaborate her influential and controversial theory of differences in men's and women's patterns of moral development. *In a Different Voice* (1982) proposed that the standard twentieth-century notion of human development as a process of individuation and autonomy applied to, and was based mostly on studies of, male development as culturally prescribed. Women, she argued, develop within an "ethic of care" in which maturity signals not isolated autonomy so much as a resolution, or at least definition, of the tension between the socially constructed role of caregiver for others and the internal discovery of a necessary care for the self.[23]

The women in Gilligan's study, in the crisis of choice, almost all tended to describe their first instinct—whether the instinct was to abort or to have the child—as "selfish." It would be selfish to refuse motherhood in order to concentrate on other desires; it would be selfish to court motherhood in order to solve problems of loneliness or to attract admiration or to put off real decision making about the relationship with the father of the child.

The nagging need to be ethically responsible to the other, the fetus, produces paralysis of self-erasure under the name of "selfishness." For one woman, Sarah, contemplating her second abortion, "what suddenly seems the responsible thing to do, namely paying for one's mistakes by having the child, suddenly appears also to be 'selfish,' bringing a child into the world 'to assuage my guilt,' " Gilligan comments, quoting Sarah (117). The morality of right (self-lessness) and wrong (selfishness) can give no guidance here, Gilligan notes, until Sarah discovers a nonnegative self that can be included in the ethic of care. Sarah decides for the abortion; just afterwards, her descriptions of her self focus on images of loss, dismemberment, dematerialization, that sundering from the hoped for whole and limitless self which marks the painful transition from Lacan's imaginary to the symbolic.

16

I just feel really beaten down, lost, and I feel really tired. There seemed to be more substance to the actual material possessions I was putting in the trunk than there was to me. . . . I am sure I did the right thing. It would have been hell for that poor kid and for me too. But I don't know if you can get what I'm getting at, because I can't get what I'm getting at. The reasons just don't fill up the whole. It's just that somehow the whole is larger than the sum of its parts when you take it apart. There is just something that happens when you put it all together that is not there when you take it apart and try to put it together, and I don't know what that is. (120–21)

Sarah's sense of the whole that disappears when you touch its parts applies, it is important to note, to being pregnant: actualizing that potential, whether by giving birth or aborting, is the termination of wholeness. As she goes through Gilligan's process, from the negative self that is "selfish" whatever choice it makes, to the stable self that both respects its own "reasons" and faces the costs of those reasons, she remembers the irrational "wholeness" which united the (potential) woman who did give birth with the (actual) woman who did not. And she constructs a new scenario for her wholeness: "If someday I have three children, I will also feel I have three children and two others that are not with us right now. I have five, and here are three of them" (121).

Both Sarah and the anonymous woman of the *Cavalier* article make the same important points. First, key to both making and accepting their choice was the "undeceived" recognition of a serious loss in the gain of abortion; and second, motherhood itself is not erased from, even perhaps is still central to, their vision of a freed self: "two magnificent daughters," "I have five, and here are three of them." These points are important, too, in the first really large-scale account of abortion stories published by Linda Bird Francke as *The Ambivalence of Abortion* in 1978, two years after her anonymous essay in *The New York Times,* "There Just Wasn't Room in Our Lives for Another Baby," evoked a huge letter-writing response containing other women's stories. Francke's own abortion story is typical of the ambivalence she records in the stories of other women she talked to and received letters from. For the first six months after the operation she felt the baby's "ghost" calling her, and she called back to it in a rapture of sorrowful defiance of the sense of limits and boundaries which had prompted the decision to abort, "Of course, we have room. Of course we do" (17). Writing the book five years later, Francke notes that "the ghost" is gone, and that the three children she already had have moved into the limitless "room" she briefly imagined in herself when the ghost first waved at her: "As my children grow and take up more and more of my time and energy, I am increasingly sure that the addition of another child for me would have been negative rather than positive" (345).

The stories Francke reports make it clear that the abortion decision is often about something other than abortion. Two examples are, with variations, repeated over and over in the case literature. In one, "Jessica," "pregnant and being shafted" by her rejecting boyfriend, reveals she had "hated (the fetus) before the abortion, but mostly I'd hated the man." Her pregnancy was for her the sign and continuation of male violence; the abortion offered escape but was followed by many months of sexual coldness which is still with her, as is her anger with men. A poignant final remark, "I live with a guy now and it's basically all right, I guess," reflects the still unresolved ambiguity not about abortion but about men (74–76). In another example, "Marigold" still struggles with the choice. Unmarried, living with her son and the young man who "dropped out of school at sixteen to get a job to take care of me," Marigold wants another baby. She had her first because "all my girlfriends was having babies and I just wanted to have one of my own, too." But she now feels it would be unfair to her boyfriend, the father, to add another child to the financially precarious household: "I'm really doing this for him." Eventually she reveals that she believes the little household could in fact take one more child if it had some support in time and energy from her own mother, who inexplicably seems to "hate" Marigold. "If I got along with my mother, then I could have this baby," she concludes, uncovering the desire to be the mother her mother is not, the mother who makes room for the child she still is (85–86).

The overarching "ambivalence" of Francke's title, however, is not

18

the one surrounding the individual's decision, but the fact that the author and the majority of those who tell their stories are simultaneously anxious that abortion be legally available, and that it not be lightly chosen. The anxiety that Luker notes can be the price of the pro-choice position is reflected in Francke's reporting that many pro-choice persons, especially some of the medical and counseling people closest to the greatest number of women having abortions, feel that legalization has "opened a Pandora's box of faulty decision making" (51). Counselors from "the Movement," trained during the illegal years to give straightforward emotional support to women in panic and fear, write Francke in 1978 that they found women "in a rush to get the abortion over with," arriving at clinics for pregnancy tests and making immediate decisions without giving their doubts time to surface (49). So counselors at clinics must develop ever more subtle techniques to probe for the conversation that the clinic patient might be hiding both from her counselor and herself, must look for the clues in body language which signal ambivalence. And when they do elicit that conversation, who is to say it is the truth? One frustrated counselor Francke talked to felt "They say what they think the counselor wants to hear just to get on with the routine. And if they have regrets or guilt later, how do you catch them?" (342). (Francke's counselor-interviewees in 1978 suffered in the initial changeover. Contemporary accounts and polls tend to stress both that women do, on the whole, make responsible decisions whether for birth or abortion, and that no counseling situation, however lengthy and subtle, can, or should, hope to erase totally the regret that may accompany a difficult moral choice, whether for abortion or birth.)

One quite unsubtle organization that arose in the 1980s to "catch" some of the women experiencing regret is WEBA, Women Exploited by Abortion. Like many right-to-life groups it has strong ties to the Roman Catholic Church, and the case histories on which its arguments ride typically include a conversion to, or recovery of, Christian faith. The book of case histories written with WEBA's help by Paula Ervin, *Women Exploited*, climaxes, to clarify its political point, with Whittaker Chamber's claim in *Witness* that a key point in "the long course of my break with Communism" came when his wife protested his casual and party-approved plan to abort her first pregnancy: "A wild joy swept me. Reason . . . the Communist Party and its theories . . . crumbled at the touch of the child" (*Witness,* 1952, reprinted in *Women Exploited,* 51).

Out of the stories her women tell, Ervin picks evidence for a number of the pro-life movement's key political claims. One is that cultural pressure is towards thoughtless abortion rather than thoughtful choice: "I wanted someone to tell me not to do this. Anyone. But no one did" (92). Another is that pro-choice medical and legal communities have deliberately misled women to believe abortion is physically and emotionally painless, without consequences. "He also assured me that there was hardly anything there. . . . I had nothing to say and felt the perfect fool for thinking I could get away with being pregnant and giving birth. The doctor was very kind, but he explained that I really had no choice but to have an abortion, even offered to tell my parents for me. This demonstrates the awesome power of the medical community in influencing life-and-death-decisions" (106). And perhaps the key philosophical and political claim here is that woman's fundamental instinct is maternal, and abortion opens a wound which only a return to maternity can heal: "It was some time afterward that I began to be healed. For a long time I didn't want children in my marriage. Maybe I felt I didn't deserve them after what I did, but after that meeting I began to want to have a child" (76).

The political bent of the book is clear, but its real structure is that of a religious romance. The heroine is Mary Magdalen, the woman who "breaks" under the stress of her withheld anguish and self-hatred to come "weeping to the feet of Christ" (18). Its hero, the one man who neither accuses nor deserts the stricken woman, who will listen to her self-accusation and validate her self-forgiveness, who figures as the divine father both of the murdered child and the murdering mother, is Jesus. Its plot returns the woman to her child self, as well as to her child, both now under the protection of the paternal figure whose New Testament iconography contains both silent welcome to the offender and (powerful inducement!) verbal chastisement to her accusers: "Let him who is without sin cast the first stone," and "Her sins, which are many, are forgiven, for she has loved much."[24]

The stories Ervin retells unveil a fundamental paradox: "Although most of the women claimed responsibility for their own action, they also felt they had been 'exploited.' But by whom? And how?" (17–18). WEBA's answer—by an atheist culture that lies about how far women can control the work of the Creator—is inadequate for many and unworkable as a basis for the law of the land. But the paradox and its question crosses all ideological boundaries in the debate. The pro-life movement's success in the mid-1980s in "capturing" this question has provoked another round of storytelling about women exploited in the bad old days (or in the case of poor women denied Medicaid funding, the bad new days) of risk, injury, and death from inept abortionists or self-induced abortions. But we can hear this paradox and this question—it was my decision, but I was exploited—by whom? how?—in these stories, too.

Many of the women in Messer and May's 1988 *Back Rooms: Voices from the Illegal Abortion Era* sought out the authors because of a feeling that their painful histories would be repeated by other women if they did not warn them by this combined telling and remembering. Some of the stories went back sixty years.

> I was 19 and I already had a child of my own. My husband was a salesman on the Lower East Side. Those were bad times. People didn't have enough money to take care of the families they had. Oh, they were married women. I never knew any single women who had abortions. (139)

Some of the stories went back thirty years: "Nancy had to claim that her mental stability was threatened by the enormous stress of her mother's impending death and her family's history of psychosis. This charade threatened to validate her worst fears; that she too might be crazy" (141). Or twenty-five years: "He said to me—I mean it was like a spy story—'I want you to pull up. I want you to get out of the car. I want you to walk purposefully. Do not look as though you are skulking or hiding'. . . . Let me tell you something—I was so desperately, from the beginning of my life, in need of attention of any kind, that this was attention to me" (46). Or just eighteen years:

> It was early 1970 and abortion was still illegal and there was nothing I could do. . . . Well, as my belly started getting bigger he started getting nutsier, and he said, 'If you can't get an abortion, I'll give you one,' and he would stand me up against the wall and throw karate kicks at me and just miss me by a quarter of an inch or just touch me. (59)

Women exploited. By whom, and how? Economic privation, male violence, a culture in which the degree of woman's departure from the careful social ("natural") track marked out for the channeling of her sexuality towards maternity is the measure of her "madness." And the living woman, trying to assemble the meaning of her personal story, may find abortion a release from these things. Or an extension of them. Or both.

The Novel: From Rape and Adultery
to Infanticide and Abortion

Adrienne Rich opens her 1976 examination of motherhood, *Of Woman Born*, with the following scene: "In a living room in 1975, I spent an evening with a group of women poets, some of whom had children. One had brought hers along, and they slept or played in adjoining rooms. We talked of poetry, and also of infanticide . . ." (4). The story they have on their minds, that of a neighbor in Massachusetts who had recently murdered her two youngest children, also forms the nucleus of her concluding chapter, "The Heart of Maternal Darkness." Here Rich argues that the violence done to women by the institution (not the biological process) which constitutes womanhood *as* motherhood, is the source of infanticidal, ultimately suicidal, rage. "Abortion is violence," she says, "a deep, desperate violence inflicted by a woman upon, first of all, herself. It is the offspring, and will continue to be the accuser, of a more pervasive and prevalent violence, the violence of rapism" (274).

So, when poets tell stories about women's lives, this is one of the stories they have to tell. They describe and ascribe the exploitation of women in a rapist culture, but they do not rejoice in abortion, even when they see it as a (temporary) release from exploitation, even when they see it as a poetically just "accuser" of the original source of violence or as a judicious use of human and female freedom. For a mysterious and often deadly necessity always shadows that freedom. Pondering the narrative of adultery in nineteenth-century fiction, critic Tony Tanner notes that divorce, the rationalist's answer to the problems of an intolerable marriage, figures in none of the key novels he studies, "nor is [divorce] felt to offer any radical solution to the problems that have arisen."[25] Nor does marriage offer any fundamental solution to the problem of rape, or abortion to the problem of maternity. True to their calling, to create characters in worlds that "signify" as well as "live," artists handling the structures of the shadow narratives—rape/seduction, adultery, infanticide/abortion—that transgress the social and contractual imperatives of marriage organize their stories towards endings— marriage or death, abortion or birth—that do not solve or resolve, only highlight, what is still radically amiss between woman and man, between woman and maternity.

This latter narrative, "the Armageddon of the maternal instinct" as Margaret Drabble will call it, comes out of Adrienne Rich's heart of maternal darkness—infanticide. In the nineteenth-century novel of infanticide lie the seeds of twentieth-century abortion narrative. And yet, before we examine this, it would be well to note briefly how often the other shadow narratives of women's lives—the narratives of rape/seduction, and adultery, or even the master narrative of courtship and marriage itself—touch on the infanticidal spirit, breathe mutinously in many disguises of the antagonism between women and maternity.

Jane Austen's master narratives of courtship and marriage, for instance, are notoriously "realistic" about, even arguably hostile to, small children. In a key moment in *Persuasion*, her sister's child "fastens himself upon" Anne Elliot's back like an incubus, bending down her back and head, and cannot be dislodged by her or his father. Anne's once and future lover finally acts to remove little Walter's throttling grasp and stifling weight, and the state of "being released from" the child begins the process of becoming reattached to the lover, finally husband.[26] *Sense and Sensibility*'s Sir John and Lady Middleton are sunk in gender roles: "Sir John was a sportsman, Lady Middleton a mother. He hunted and shot and she humoured her children." The children are little monsters who "pulled her about, tore her clothes, and" (what is surely key to this and every woman writer) "put an end to every kind of discourse except what related to themselves" (1258).

"Matrimony, as the origin of change, was always disagreeable" to Emma Woodhouse's father (764), and she, alone among Austen's heroines in *choosing* not to marry, is her father's daughter. Mr. Knightley thinks Emma's antipathy to marriage "means just nothing at all" (765), but Emma, understanding very well that her society will not look down on a *wealthy* old maid, insists that she is perfectly content to work off her erotic desires in making other people's matches and to supply herself with "objects of affection" from her sister's steadily increasing brood, preferring the "comfort" of the cooler aunthood to the throttling heat ("what is warmer and blinder") of motherhood (815).

And *Wuthering Heights*'s Cathy dies in childbed after the birth of her child confirms the final loss of the "half-savage and hardy and free" being she was herself before marriage.[27] The crowd of foster mothers in the Victorian novel generally signifies not only the true state of maternal mortality in the nineteenth century but also the subliminal sense of the whole culture that pregnancy has in it a death as well as a life.

The classic novels of rape advert to this same fatality. In Richardson's *Clarissa*, six weeks after the heroine is raped, the discourse turns breathlessly to the possibility of pregnancy. The perpetrator hopes for it, the victim's hateful family suspends its discussions until they know what to them would be the deserved "worst" punishment for the daughter's independence. Pregnancy would propel the victim toward marriage, or at least toward life, however compromised; it would make immoral the death the heroine passionately desires. In a novel where erotic energy and writing fury seem forms of one another, pregnancy and birth would enable the rapist's "pen" to permanently inscribe the victim's page. Outwriting Lovelace three pages to his every one in the final volumes, Clarissa wrests back the page of her self from his pen, steadily eluding the answer to the "cruel" question of her possible pregnancy, affirming that her death will be the answer. Her answer to herself, in an inset page stitched to the letter of inquiry with black silk, conflates the image of divine metamorphosis with human pregnancy and birth: "Yet all the days of my appointed time will I wait till my change come."[28]

Hardy's Tess also figures as a blank page upon which her rapist traces a "coarse pattern" (63) impossible to erase or rewrite, though she tries, poignantly, to regrow the "tissue" of maidenhead as one would regrow the skin over other kinds of wounds.[29] Alec's rape of Tess is confirmed by pregnancy, and the resulting birth, harmonizing with natural law but outraging social law, is accompanied by a maternal wish both infanticidal and suicidal, though at that time only the baby, not the mother, ends up in the graveyard. Five years and three hundred still inscribed pages later, Tess dies for killing her seducer, a desperate act in which she tried unsuccessfully to escape the original rape inscription that defined her as "Mrs. Alec D'Urberville" despite her marriage in law and in spirit to Angel Clare.

The pregnant child-Tess cried out to her mother, "Why didn't you warn me? Ladies know what to fend hands against, because they read novels that tell them of these tricks; but I never had the choice o' learning in that way, and you did not help me" (72). But Tess's concept of the novel as a woman's book of rules, a guide to safe sex in marriage, is in error, argues Tony Tanner. Though the eighteenth- and nineteenth-century novel makes a conscious and conscientious move toward "marriage and the securing of genealogical continuity" in birth, its narrative energy, says Tanner, is increasingly about departures from that line of progress, especially that departure called adultery, which involves "the decomposition of that unstable, supposedly unitary, trinity, the wife-mother-lover" (4).

Tolstoy's Anna Karenina, for instance, decomposes in the first months of adulterous passion. She has always known her wifehood for a role, but now that "partly sincere but greatly exaggerated role of a mother living for her son that she had assumed" became transparent, too.[30] The son of her husband is a "compass" which showed Anna and her lover, Vronsky, the degree of their "divergence from the right course" (170). Pregnant with the daughter of her lover, Anna dreams the clearest foreshadowing of her desire for death until, at the fetus's quickening, that partly sincere but still greatly exaggerated role of motherhood replaces the horror with "blissful attention" (329). Soon even the role of Vronsky's lover becomes a round of mechanical passion—love, possessive jealousy, guilty despair—and Anna literally loses track of who she is. Neither Kerenin's son, nor Vronsky's daughter, can be the compass now. The dissolving boundaries of "family" stir an incestuous vision, one last desire that the two beings she loves "equally," her son and her lover, be united in one erotic object (580). She desires nothing that can be, a desire figured in the scene (surely meant to be shocking) where Anna announces to her naive sister-in-law that, with information (on birth control and abortifacients presumably) provided by her doctor, she will have no more children (577–79).

Interestingly, Hawthorne's Hester Prynne, claiming with the narrative's own authority that her adulterous passion "had a consecration all its own," faces the same impossible double desire, to unite her lover and their child in one erotic object.[31] When the three finally meet in the forest and Hester tries to compose an outlaw "family" from their elements, an invisible wall seems to rise between the child, who is the scarlet "A," and the lovers who wear, and did, that deadly and consecrated writing. "The family," centered on that glimmering fantasy creature, the wife-mother-lover, and the child, who is at once "the Pearl of great price" and "the freedom of a broken law," literally cannot exist in the same world. When Hester takes up again the cast-aside scarlet "A," the almost repudiated child, she sets in motion the death of her lover. And the death of the lover, Hawthorne's narrator says, restores "humanity" to the elfin child whose retreat from freedom to the standard training and behavior of a nineteenth-century romantic heroine seems to reknit the broken law of matrimony: at least Pearl's illegitimacy mysteriously forms no bar to her contracting marriage with a nobleman across the sea. More deeply, Pearl's final enclosure in romantic marriage signals the (fantastic) return of the novel's world to the "right track" of channeled female sexuality; both Pearl's and Hester's disturbingly lawless erotic fields disappear. Once again the child was "the compass."

A still deeper law is at stake in the novels of seduction which lead to maternal infanticide and mothers in custody, the law not only of matrimony but of maternity broken. Mrs. Frances Trollope's *Jessie Phillips*, which at first glance might be the very model of Arnold's newspaper paragraph, "Wragg is in Custody," evades the terror of this outlawry, this freedom, at the last moment. While the beautiful Jessie did indeed bear a child to Frederick Dalton and walk out from the workhouse with it, her trial for infanticide reveals that it was in fact the vile father who kicked it to death, finding it momentarily laid down by the wretched but adoring mother.[32] Walter Scott's *Heart of Midlothian* does not evade so much as displace the act of maternal infanticide. Though Effie Deans bore a child to the seducer, George Staunton-Robertson, and remembers having infanticidal fantasies ("bad thoughts put in my mind by the Enemy"), the novel reveals at last that the child was stolen and given to gypsies (that nineteenth-century narrative nursery) by a woman later hanged for a witch.[33] This woman had, however, murdered her own daughter, Madge Wildfire, child by the same seducer, the year before. In the complex dynamic of victimized and rivalrous sisterhood by which the two young mothers are linked, the specter of maternal infanticide is raised around Effie, displaced to Madge, and finally located in her mother, Meg Murdockson. The drawing of the innocent (and sexless) heroine, Jeanie Deans, into this dynamic occurs at a spooky mountain cairn built over the body of a woman who had had her throat cut, for no discernible reason, by her husband. Thus does the novel, instinctively if deviously, connect (without condoning) maternal infanticide with male gynocide.

Scott's novel turns on an old point of Scottish law so suspicious of mothers that it requires no evidence of birth or body to hang for infanticide. Rather, the accused must "prove the negative"—prove, in the absence of witnessed birth or body, that she did make active plans to bear and care for the child she was only suspected of having conceived, specifically by "communicating her condition," admitting her sexual outlawry, to the matrons of the town. Effie, convicted, though not guilty, is eventually freed by a pardon from royal authorities touched by a plea from her sister, Jeanie.[34]

George Eliot's Hetty Sorrel, convicted and guilty of infanticide, is freed at the very foot of the gallows by a pardon obtained by her seducer, Arthur Donnithorne. Unlike Hawthorne's Hester, Eliot's Hester has little nobility of character; like Scott's Effie, Eliot's Hetty deeply mistrusted the ability of the community of good women, especially the "good sister" that Dinah Morris tried to be to her, and relied on her man to set things right by marriage. Like Effie, she had infanticidal fantasies that grew out of suicidal ones. But here in *Adam Bede*, her first full-length novel, George Eliot looks more closely at the heart of maternal darkness than Scott. Though at the crisis the pregnant Hetty sought a pool to drown herself in, she found that her love of her own life was too strong. It would have to be the baby's life instead. Though Hetty is aware of a wish only to hide, not specifically to drown, the baby under the water, under the compassionate probing of Dinah Morris she admits she momentarily hated the pregnancy and the resulting baby: "It was like a heavy weight hanging round my neck."[35]

George Eliot's highly masculinized narrator ("God preserve you and me from being the beginners of such misery," "he" says to "his" male readers. [374]) worships motherhood, certainly: "The mother's yearning, that completest type of the life in another life which is the essence of real human love, feels the presence of the cherished child even in the debased, degraded man." But in a startling reversal, the "mother" who represents that type in this passage is the male hero, Adam Bede, and Hetty is the degraded "man": "And to Adam, this pale, hard-looking culprit was the Hetty who had smiled at him in the garden under the apple tree" (415).

If motherhood is the type of Eliot's major moral principle, "life in another life," infanticide is the type of minor principle that also informs all her work—irrevocableness. Though Adam Bede's suffering at the first news of Arthur's seduction of Hetty is the first "embodiment of what Arthur must shrink from believing in—the irrevocableness of his own wrong doing" (300)—the ultimate embodiment of the deed that cannot be undone, the last "word" that cannot be unspoken, is the dead body of Hetty's child, denied but born, buried but found. Here, where the refusal of life in another life meets the denial that acts have irrevocable consequences, is the heart of Eliot's moral universe. "Nature" and culture, too, "irrevocably" give this primary role, representing life in another life, to the female. Eliot's art tries to extend it to Adam and to all humanity, though the price here is the erasure of Hetty's female nature in the masculinized "hardness" of her "culprit" face, the face that denies irrevocableness. Here, too, is the heart of nineteenth-century narrative, which moves ever to the speech that shatters the veils of concealment, the detailing of the "irrevocable."

Twentieth-century narrative, discovering silence and less certain of its power or mission to define what lies beneath the veil, might be imagined to be naturally attracted away from the more obvious plots of rape and adultery to the more equivocal scene of abortion narrative, which depicts the undoing of the not yet done, which makes known the denial of the never fully knowable. An interesting example of this drawing, I would argue, occurs in Virginia Woolf's *Between the Acts*.[36] The machinery and the reality of the rape plot and the adultery plot haunt the pages of this novel of a June day in 1939, where the people of a village gather at the manor house to watch a historical pageant. But the novel seems at its elliptical center actually to be about the attempt, and the failure, "to bring a common meaning to birth." " 'Abortive' was the word that expressed her" (15), says the narrative of its heroine, the wife, mother, lover, lady of the manor, Isa Oliver.

Isa feels both defined and confined by her gender roles. She writes her poetry in a journal bound like a domestic account book for fear of ridicule by the stockbroker husband, "the father of my children," whom she both mocks and clings to with that talismanic phrase. Her poems, her being, are unfinished, they sink in midflight. Like most of the others who come to the pageant given on her grounds, she seeks the "unacted part," the limitless role, she feels somehow born to play. She tries one on in her mind, the adulterous wife, as she feels her body respond erotically to a neighboring "gentleman farmer," but that very phrase, also edged with mockery, alienates her from the role, so routinized in its Byronic melodies, its Tolstoyan aftermath.

Cliché is the word for both the role and the feeling, stirred either by the "gentleman farmer" or "the father of my children" (14). But two other things seem "real" as the novel opens: her nameless feeling for her little boy (14) and a passage she reads in *The Times* of that June day, 1939:

> The trooper told her the horse had a green tail; but she found it was just an ordinary horse. And they dragged her up to the barrack room where she was thrown upon a bed. Then one of the troopers removed part of her clothing and she screamed and hit him about the face. (20)

This narrative of rape, contained in a newspaper with which her father-in-law had, masking himself with it like a beaked beast, just terrified Isa's little boy, lodges itself in Isa's brain. "The brawl in the barrack room where they stripped her naked" (156) becomes part of "the burden . . . laid on me in the cradle, . . . crooned by singing women; what we must remember, what we would forget" (155). The image is of a burden that can neither be abandoned nor relieved by birth, of woman's life as an uncompletable pregnancy: " 'Kneel down,' said the past. 'Fill your pannier from our trees. Rise up, donkey, go your way till your heels blister and your hoofs crack' " (155).

What Woolf's narrative doesn't tell us is the reason this narrative hit the newspapers that June day (and it was 1938, the year of writing, not 1939). The reason was abortion. The fourteen-year-old girl in this true story, pregnant after the rape, had provided what Dr. Aleck Bourne, fellow of the Royal College of Surgeons, called a "God-given opportunity" to test English law on abortion. On 14 June 1938, with the permission of her parents and other doctors, he performed an abortion and submitted to arrest. The resulting trial and acquittal began the process of abortion law reform in England.[37]

For Woolf the omission of this side of the story was probably less a matter of prudent concealment than a wish to delocalize the matter of abortion. In this narrative abortive is the word for almost everything: roles, poems, pageant, relationships, ideas, swell and disappear without clearly discernible birth or fruit in a world made bearable only by the shimmer of meaningfulness forever being dispersed and by the telling of the truth about this dispersal. The old plots of marriage, rape, adultery still beckon the mind, even compel the flesh, with their vision of process, completeness: "Before they slept, they must fight; after they had fought, they would embrace. From that embrace, another life might be born." But Isa and the narrator are tired of these plots: "Love and hate—how they tore one asunder! Surely it was time someone invented a new plot . . . " (215).

*

When I first planned this study, I thought perhaps somebody had invented a new plot, but the plot of maternal choice is not simply another variation on love and hate. Certainly it does not form the plot Woolf seems to have been looking for, the one which builds itself around peace, the third, hardly examined, of the three emotions—love, hate, peace—"which made the ply of human life" (92). Some narratives achieve rest in a stance about abortion and choice, but not peace. Nor is it new. Patriarchal infanticide is as old as *Oedipus Rex*. The ballad of woman at odds with maternity certainly predates the anonymous fifteenth-century tale of "Mary Hamilton," royal mistress, infanticide, "hanged in Edinbro' Town," the chosen narrating persona of Woolf herself in *A Room of One's Own*. And the abortion plot as sentimental climax was already old when William Goldman's would-be producer tells his would-be playwright in *Boys and Girls Together* (1964) that *"there better not be a big abortion scene*—I'm bored with them already."[38]

The producer was thinking, perhaps, of Hemingway's "Hills like White Elephants," or Faulkner's *As I Lay Dying*, or Barth's *End of the Road*, or Lorraine Hansberry's *A Raisin in the Sun*, all of which I treat in the following chapters. Or other stories I might have treated: Dreiser's *An American Tragedy* (1925), where Clyde Griffith, turned away by the druggists and doctors of Lycurgus and Schenectady when he seeks an abortion for his unloved lover, Roberta, is moved to solve the problem by murder. Or Richard Yates's *Revolutionary Road* (1961), whose timidly manipulative antihero, Frank Wheeler, hating yet afraid to abandon the empty routines of suburban "family life," first forces his wife away from the safe abortion that might have freed them both for a richer more demanding life, then, as love dies between them, exits wishing brutally that she had insisted on the abortion. She performs the abortion on herself and dies of it. Or John Updike's *Rabbit, Run* (1960), whose skittish boy-man,

Harry Angstrom, impregnates his wife, runs away to a mistress and impregnates her, returns to his wife for the daughter's birth, returns to his mistress as wife and baby come back home. As the novel ends, Rabbit mourns the baby daughter his wife drunkenly drowned at his departure, and yet decides not to return to the mistress who has given him an ultimatum—marriage, or she will abort their child. Updike's 1981 *Rabbit is Rich* shows aging Rabbit, nineteen years later, fixated on the idea of a nubile, illegitimate daughter. Though the revisited mistress, Ruth, swears she had the abortion and challenges him to look at the birth certificate which will prove Annabelle too young for the role, Rabbit refuses to look, preferring what he has always longed for, "the vibration of excitement, of possibility untested."[39] The novel ends, ominously enough, with Rabbit claiming his infant granddaughter as "his."

Or, quite likely, the producer had in mind Broadway blockbusters like Sidney Kingsley's 1949 *Detective Story,* whose rigidly moralistic hero pursues an illegal abortionist, unaware that his wife had once had to make use of him. Or wildly popular best-sellers like Grace Metalious's 1956 *Peyton Place,* where an abortion performed by the well-liked town doctor on the incestuously raped ingenue, Selena Cross, becomes the hidden material of the climactic trial in which Selena is tried for the murder of her stepfather.

Where abortion is not simply a sentimental climax but a part of the choice raised by contemplating the whole vexed process of human sexuality and maternity, contemporary writers are as conflicted as feminism itself, no less so after choice is legal than when it was an outlaw choice. There is wide agreement on the desire to erase the woman's death, or brush with death, as the necessary complement to the sexuality that results in pregnancy; but for many, death, some kind of death, the death of something, hums in the air around abortion itself.

I have chosen to work with novels by John Barth and Margaret Drabble in my first chapter to set up some paradigms about human and artistic, male and female, choice. Barth is a compelling figure for this paradigm, both because his novels create worlds in which women are maneuvered toward the abortion that never really represents their choice, and because he has been a key contemporary spokesperson for the pervasiveness, the inevitability, of the fictive in all choice. In Barth's *The End of the Road* and more directly in *Sabbatical*, we see "the father," the first person narrator of the story, literally turn abortion into art, bringing forth men children only.

The contemporary woman's novel, in several senses, has grown up with Margaret Drabble, whose early *The Millstone* and more recent *The Middle Ground* I will study here. She is *the* reporter on contemporary, quotidian, female middle-class life, and, as I shall argue, no stranger, despite (because of) her commitment to the realistic tradition of Austen and Eliot, to the fictiveness of all "pattern." Both novelists returned to the matter of pregnancy and choice after legalization in the 1980s not because they changed their minds, but to develop plots less tragic, more subtle, about the losses and gains of the new freedom. Margaret Atwood, whose early *Surfacing*, as we shall see, depicts a situation in which abortion is male manipulation, later depicted in *The Handmaid's Tale* (1985) a society in which abortion is once again the hallmark of a rebel underground of freedom during an age of compulsory pregnancy. Marge Piercy, whose *Braided Lives*, set in the fifties and sixties, fought fiercely for abortion rights, has recently published *Gone to Soldiers* (1987), set during World War II and the Holocaust. Here, one of the protagonists, a Holocaust survivor, advises a pregnant niece of her free choice. But the weight of the text suggests that Naomi will bring her pregnancy to term symbolically enough in Israel; the fetus is linked with the beloved, dead twin-self, killed by the Nazis, ready to be reborn. These artists haven't changed their minds either. They simply have located the endangered moral principle of female selfhood, with its "ethic of care," differently in these later books.

Women writers using maternal choice plots find themselves almost inevitably engaged with two special problems waiting in the very nature of language and narrative to help shape the plots. One of them has been beautifully set forth by Barbara Johnson in an essay in *Diacritics* called "Apostrophe, Animation, and Abortion." It is the nature of consciousness to address what is presented to it; it is the inevitable nature of female consciousness to address its pregnancy. "Because of the ineradicable tendency of language to animate whatever it addresses," Johnson notes, "rhetoric itself can always have already answered 'yes' to the question of whether a fetus is a human."[40] In the abortion poems by women poets Johnson has studied, a further paradoxical narrative move seems inevitable. If the address animates a being inside, then it is the inside being of the speaker herself which is first animated with that ineradicable yes, and then abandoned, erased, or set aside by the described abortion. In lyric poetry, as Johnson points out, the poet can both have the abortion and evade the hum of death, even when the abortion is dramatized as the woman's choice: "Each of these poems exists, finally, *because* a child does not" (36). Within the brief frame of the lyric address to the dead fetus, the fetus lives.

The novels I have studied, almost without exception, contain lyric moments of address to the fetus or what the fetus represents or represented, as well as, where the narrative chose birth rather than abortion, to or by the child. But in a novel these lyric moments are caught up in a long narrative of dailiness, of consciousness returning to uncertainty, animation going dull, of consciousness anticipating consequences, and plot confirming or disconfirming the anticipation. And here is where the second problem enters. The multiple addresses of consciousness in a long prose narrative render consciousness itself a subject. The conscious dramatization of birth or abortion as a choice moves maternity itself out of the realm of instinct and into the realm of consciousness. "When a woman speaks about the death of children in any sense other than that of pure loss," Johnson notes, "a powerful taboo is violated" (38), not only because of the archetypal, patriarchal reliance upon women to say yes to the child (and no to the poem) but more deeply because of the archetypal reliance of all humans upon an instinct which operates below consciousness, ignorant of choice. This is the real reason why abortion, and the consciousness it brings to a new depth is "the Armageddon of the maternal instinct": these are the last days, not of maternity, but of maternity as instinct.

This is partly why I have chosen Joan Didion's *Play It as It Lays*, Margaret Atwood's *Surfacing*, Mary Gordon's *The Company of Women*, and Marge Piercy's *Braided Lives* as material for my second chapter, on women writers. All these novels take up the matter of

34

maternal choice ultimately through the anguished and devious, sometimes "mad," filter of first person consciousness, where consciousness hides from itself until it can hide no longer.

Male writers have imagined their way into the pregnancy/birth scene for millennia, sometimes with terrifying gusto. In *The Prisoner of Sex*, Norman Mailer hymned "the art of the egg,"[41] bemoaned "the lost gravity of the act" since pregnancy ceased to involve the risk of death (93), and longed for "the days of honest abortion when the fingernails of the surgeon were filthy and the heart of a woman went screaming through a cave as steel scraped at the place where she touched the beyond" (49–50). Few male writers blaspheme/sacralize/envy the womb in quite that direct a way. Yet even the least "masculinized" writers bring with them to the plot of maternal choice a sensitivity to the special exposures of the male psyche before the fact of its own powerlessness in the completion of the creation of life. For Hemingway before Mailer, pregnancy/birth was woman's battlefield, her territory of the bull, the only possible place in which to experience the valor that is true being. Faulkner might mock the sensitive Quentin Compson's balancing of the "whole vast globy earth" of his honor on the unviolated maidenhead of his sister, Caddy. Yet the male's Oedipal sense simultaneously of insideous corruption by, and terrible exclusion from, the world represented by female sexuality and maternity colors all his work. In more contemporary novels by John Barth (chapter 1) and Thomas Keneally, Graham Swift, and John Irving (chapter 3) we can see the fears of the father laid bare, along with the demonic compensations, from murder to incest to the word itself, which he invents in his powerlessness.

Finally, in chapter 4, I take up, with some hesitation, the scene of black maternity as described by contemporary, black American women writers. As a white feminist listening to the warnings of black feminists over the past ten years, I have sometimes felt simultaneously forbidden to exclude and forbidden to include the work and issues of black women writers. Barbara Smith remarked in 1977 that "when white women look at Black women's works they are of course ill-equipped to deal with the subtleties of racial politics."[42] Of course. Barbara Christian, in her important, first full-length treatment of black women writers in 1980, everywhere suggests that the process named in her first section, "From Stereotype to Character," applies to the perception of white citizens, novelists, and critics as well.[43] Yet Smith and Christian, like Gwendolyn Brooks, Lorraine Hansberry, Toni Morrison, Alice Walker, Gloria Naylor, and Gayle Jones, have equipped all of us better in the meantime. This study concludes with an examination of black women writers' work not because of some project of "inclusion" but because many of the stereotypes and issues closest to the heart of that work, the "contented mammy," the "tragic mulatto," the displacement of the black baby by the white in the system of patriarchal slavery and its aftermath, are close to the heart of this study.

For in many ways the dilemmas of black maternity form the clearest index to that civil war within, the Armageddon of the maternal instinct. Nowhere else is the culturally prescribed alienation of the maternal body from the human "subject" who is present there so clearly depicted. Nowhere else can we so intimately see the way in which *either* birth, stubbornly carried through despite the simultaneous entry of the child into shared slavery with the mother, *or* abortion, stubbornly chosen in order to deny "the man" his "property," may well be an act of radical, and even maternal, self-affirmation. For it is not only the fecund "mamas" of Lorraine Hansberry's *A Raisin in the Sun* and Gloria Naylor's *The Women of Brewster Place* who evoke and momentarily represent the "lost territory" of the plenteous maternal self, cells dividing and splitting without a gap or lack. It is also the aborting and abandoning mother of Alice Walker's *Meridian* and the murdering madonna of Toni Morrison's *Beloved* whose very choice of loss somehow pulls them, and us, into a more mystic domain of healing beyond the loss/gain–presence/absence dichotomy in which our reason still imprisons us. From these works, too, closest of all to the heart of maternal darkness, come the most astonishing invitations to feel hope.

1

Paradigms for the Plot of Maternal Choice: Novels by John Barth and Margaret Drabble

T he plot involving maternal choice provides at one level irresistible material, even a paradigm, for the storyteller. The
character, the narrative, proceeding down the paths of
her/his desire under the illusion of free will, disappears into an ancient, immalleable process, pulled into a story old as organisms. The
story had one end. Now, if it can have two, it can have twenty;
choice is restored as reality. The choosing hand of the storyteller was
always evident in the impregnation. Man and woman mate, yes,
but a pregnancy? Why now? Why with him? Science has ideas, but
the storyteller has the reason; pregnancy punishes sex, rewards
love, metonymizes, analogizes growth. Birth valorizes change. And
death? Relieves punishment, ironizes reward, denies growth or offers another route to it. If from one feminist point of view the
sacralization of birth is a plot of the patriarchy to extend itself
through progeny, from another the sacralization of abortion
amounts to a variation of that same woman-abusing story: a way to
gain total sexual access while leading the woman to control the
product of the womb in what men have defined as women's
interest.

Both as social drama and as narrative paradigm, the maternal
choice plot offers rich possibilities in three linked actions or relationships: the woman and her lover becomes the woman and her
potential/actual child becomes the woman and her (or isn't it his?)
doctor. The storyteller, who once hid within the natural "order" of
miscarriage or the unnatural "order" of infanticide if s/he wanted
the transcendent leaven of death in the plot, now stands revealed

with the characters as the maker of the choice that kills the not chosen, illuminating as never before the processes and the obliquely terrifying results of choice.

I have chosen two apparently unlike authors to begin this study of novelists and the topos of abortion. Margaret Drabble is an Englishwoman writing in the realist tradition of Jane Austen and George Eliot. John Barth is an American man helping to construct the post-realist tradition of mid-twentieth-century philosophical fabulism. Each, however, has written two books centering on abortion, one before and one after the legalization of abortion. In all four books the protagonists are writers and critics; as such the protagonist/narrators, the implied authors, are sharply conscious of the artifice involved when humans lay hands on the story of pregnancy. Abortion ends three of the four stories. One ends in agony, but all of them end in some kind of woe. Even the pregnancy carried to term, moving to its own story, brings its quantum of loss.

In these four first person narratives, hyperconsciousness struggles with instinct, maternal or paternal. Drabble's female speakers are pregnant "by accident"; so are the women Barth's male speakers impregnate. But paradigms of choice emerge from the scenes of these accidents. For pregnancy seems in all four cases also linked to some psychic instinct in the women to find and cherish, or bitterly relinquish, or soberly consider, a lost or as yet unformed element of self. And impregnation is linked to some psychic instinct in the men, too, to write with the body of woman the received script of manhood. Drabble's women draw back from their impregnators immediately and permanently to construct virtually alone the maternal body that is theirs and to ponder the consequences of their choice of birth (*The Millstone*, 1965) or abortion (*The Middle Ground*, 1980) for that maternity. Barth's women implicate their men in that choice (that is, Barth thrusts his men into his women's choices) from start to finish, collapsing the whole structure of heterosexual romance, and psycho-social "reality" as well, into abortion and maternal death (*The End of the Road*, 1958) or restoring these structures as fragile, emphatically paternal fictions (*Sabbatical*, 1982).

John Barth: The Game, the Gun, and the Mask

John Barth's *The End of the Road* is one of the half-dozen most painful books I have ever read, not least because as a literary critic, the implied reader of the tale, I am deeply implicated in the exhilarating "duel of articulations" (112) which characterizes, which *is* the character of, the male antagonists.[1] And yet "what was a game for [the men] was a terrible fight" for the female protagonist (63). The men control experience, above all relationships, by turning it into speech: "To turn experience into speech—that is, to classify, to categorize, to conceptualize, to grammarize, to syntactify it—is always a betrayal of experience, a falsification of it: but only so betrayed can it be dealt with at all, and only in so dealing with it did I ever feel a man, alive and kicking" (112). At the primary level of the narrative, the woman, Rennie, *is* experience itself, awaiting grammarization, transformation, betrayal. Resisting the narrator's categorization just a trifle, we can see experience, woman, the person Rennie, controlling/disrupting speech by turning it into pregnancy. Married to one man—Joe, the American pragmatist, is writing a Ph.D. dissertation on the saving roles of innocence and energy in American political and economic history during the narrative—Rennie goes to bed once with another—Jake, the French existentialist and narrator, has completed his M.A. in English but halted before the task of the thesis, unable to prefer one thesis to another literarily or philosophically. What results, her articulation of her dilemma, is a pregnancy she will not accept. So she says. Forced past speech by this twist of the plot, this eruption of an ancient story, the men supply, each from his characteristic arsenal, solutions: Joe, a gun (American innocence and energy); Jake, his own therapist, mythotherapist, who becomes, obliging Rennie's myth, an abortionist. In the novel's grim climax Rennie dies on the abortionist's table in a strangely determined way, struggling against the sharp curette ("She's cutting herself to pieces!"), leaning into the oxygen mask "as though anxious to lose consciousness," finally vomiting and aspirating into her lungs under the mask the contents of a big dinner her husband had prepared for her ("She should've known better" [180–82]). And the pointless verdict rendered by the doctor— "This thing was everybody's fault, let it be everybody's lesson" (183)—gives way to the appalling probability that "this" was in fact everybody's solution, even, beneath her mask, terminated through a pregnancy for which there is no narrative proof but her own fatal contention, Rennie's.

Probability is of course the only thing we have, philosophically or narratively, in Barth's game of a novel, where the characters all see themselves proudly as starting from ethical scratch, from personal zero, in the task of building patterns, absolutes, to live by. Since no value is absolute in itself, any value chosen as such may be an individual's absolute; thus, choice is the absolute value. Joe, the American pragmatist, has chosen as his value/pattern the "completely honest" marriage of two independent persons he (thinks he) has with Rennie. By completely honest, of course, he means that every experience must be turned into speech between them, and Rennie's independence, he allows, will be a little longer in the building than his, since he was the original articulator of the pattern. Indeed, as evidence of his godlike intention to develop free will and independence in his wife, he takes her "seriously" enough to knock her cold when she takes other people's points of view seriously, even his (43–44). Their marriage (they have two children) has been a success on these principles, since the woman, fatally attracted by this monomyth of "being taken seriously," remodeled herself, being taken.

Into this heaven comes the devil, Jake Horner, a man of like stamp with the pragmatist god, Joe. Jake has come to the same philosophical zero as Joe has. Lacking both the innocence and the energy that allowed Joe to choose a relative value and act on it with utter consistency, as if it were an absolute, Jake suffers the consequence—immobility. He has been "remobilized" by a mysterious, black doctor, a figure out of the confidence man fable of American letters who offers him ways of choosing actions, making decisions, by "scripting" scenes and characters for him to play and to enforce on others. His facility at scripting gives him both a writer's glee and a writer's guilt. Scenes in Jake's classrooms (the Wily Articulator and the Bewildered Teens) and in the bedroom of fellow English teacher

Peggy Rankin (the Young Stud and the Forty-Year-Old-Pickup) "play" with scripted consistency and comic élan.

Scenes with Rennie and Joe Morgan are harder for him to script, not only because Jake begins to desire Rennie, as Joe originally had, for the "clumsy force" (47), the unarticulated existence which radiates from her strong body and restless mind, but also because his glee and guilt are no match for Joe's energy and innocence. Jake's hold on any one script is fragile; both his writerly glee and writerly guilt incline him to slide from one script to another, to another. Joe's innocence, on the other hand, keeps him to his one chosen as-if pattern, and his demonic energy impels him and everyone caught in his script to live that pattern down to the last terrible point of its logic—a deadly pro-choice. He is, as Jake jokes (in vain), a Boy Scout, and he will get that old lady across the street if it kills both of them.

Caught between these rival masquemakers, Rennie seizes a competing script of her own, ancient, manichaean, with a special, female twist. As the arbitrary maker of their universe, Joe is "God" for her, but out of his innocence and energy "God" has "conjured up the Devil" (63) to test his own strength and hers. But now there are two masters, scripters, in the world. Which is the source and which the artifact? Which is "real?" The one who can make her pregnant. "Then," as she tells Jake the myth she daydreamed, "[Joe] made me pregnant again so I'd know he was the one who was real and I wouldn't be scared and so—I'd grow to be just as strong as he is, and stronger than somebody who isn't even real" (63).

It seems quite possible that Rennie invents this impregnation, desperately seeking Joe as reality while her faith in him, in the bitter consistency of his mask with his self, collapses.[2] That evening Jake persuades Rennie to spy on her husband with him when Joe is alone. She protests that "real people aren't any different when they're alone. No masks. What you see of them is authentic." But Joe *is* different. The Boy Scout masturbates, struts in goosesteps, speaks in mask-bending multisyllables: "Sklurching up his eye corners, zbluggling his mouth about, glubing his cheeks. Mither Morgle. Nyong Nyang Nyumpie. Vglibble-vglobble vglup. Vgliggy *bloo!* Thlucky thlucky, thir" (66). The consequence for Rennie is

41

utter disorientation, a "fall" into sex with Jake, then a continuation of sex with both god and the devil because god insists, consistent with his principles, that she stay in the situation until she can choose, and clearly articulate her reasons for choosing, one side or the other. And the final consequence is pregnancy. Both men used condoms, "same brand, as a matter of fact," and Rennie, the last reported pregnancy by Joe having been admittedly "wishful thinking," is "pretty late . . . vomiting a lot" and "sure" she's pregnant this time, because she doesn't want to be (143).

In the novel's iconography, the pregnancy is accompanied by, makes visible, actually is, a gun, a Colt .45, which Joe digs out of the basement when he first hears about the "romantic triangle" and keeps with him at all times in case his position should finally require that he, or someone, should use it. The gun links the male rivals as lovers. Casually, anticipating Gayle Rubin's diagnosis of the erotic triangle as traffic in women designed to bring men together, Jake muses, "That statement thrilled me. Perhaps it was Joe Morgan, after all, that I loved" (140).

The gun's appearance also marks a dire but, in its corrupt way, welcome change in the plot. The game as duel of articulations is stalemated two-thirds of the way through the novel. When Joe lays the gun on a table in the center of the "perfect equilateral triangle" formed by the three seated protagonists, he invokes the profoundest rule of story. Barth is fond of the rule; he will invoke and play with Chekhov's formulation of it in *Sabbatical:* "A pistol hung on the wall in Act One must be fired in Act Three."[3]

Finally, the gun is a triumphant sign, male sign, surely, even in Ibsen's *Hedda Gabler,* even in Flannery O'Connor's "A Good Man Is Hard to Find," that the highest philosophical-theological stakes are on the table. Facing or using the gun is, at last, taking/being taken seriously. "She'd of been a good woman if it had been somebody there to shoot her every day of her life," morosely opines the divine criminal of the human woman in O'Connor's 1955 story.[4] And *only* if somebody is there to shoot her. This is, terribly, the inevitable, consistent, final position of the man committed to a value, even (especially) a value which he has artificially inflated by pragmatic free choice into an absolute. Joe Morgan's passionate argument, as Rennie reaches for the gun to shoot herself rather than bear a child (possibly, to the devil) is that only *he* loves her enough to let her make, and take, this lonely, exalted decision. Jake, appalled at this deadly truth, pushes "value" away with the gun and offers the alternative—abortion.

The last mile of *The End of the Road* is Jake's frantic, black-comic search for an abortionist in the white Maryland suburbs of the 1950s. He dons, with the ease of the practiced if desperate scripter, the necessary mask of "Henry Dempsey," whose wife's doctor, "Dr. Joseph Banks" (also himself), certifies that "Mrs. Dempsey" will go homicidally, suicidally mad if forced to bring a third baby to term. The whirlwind of storytelling and masquerading finally persuades a local doctor to set up the "really competent abortion done in a good hospital by a good obstetrician," which is the only kind of abortion that Joe will allow. Otherwise, Joe reflects (or is it his desire?), "The only abortion she could get would be a half-ass job by some half-ass doctor who could mess her up for the rest of her life" (148).

This script requires Rennie Morgan's cooperation as "Mrs. Henry Dempsey," however, and Rennie, displaying "a great unanimity of spirit" with the candid god of her marriage, refuses the saving mask: "I won't tell lies or assent to lies, and I won't pretend to be anybody but myself" (161). This, as Jake the existentialist and Barth the fabulist know, is an untenable position for a living human being, whose "self" is multiple and inevitably composed of fictions, lies. But the single self that Rennie Morgan has decided to be wants the truth, the decisiveness, the healing (deadly) finality of the gun, not the masks. When, in utter desperation, Jake sells himself to the mysterious, black doctor who has been his mephistophelian re-mobilizer and therapist in exchange for his promise to perform the abortion with no lies, no masks, both Morgans are disappointed. Jake had "spoiled something" (176), the perfect philosophical no exit/no choice situation that justifies, consolidates, the notion of absolute value.

What makes the doctor mephistophelian, of course, is that he gives all the characters exactly what they want, or, as the syntax of the narrative makes clear, allows them to take what they want. He is the articulator and teacher of "mythotherapy"—the science of choosing roles, reconceiving scripts, donning masks (but if you don two, then they must be compatible masks, like choosing to be Odysseus disguised as a swineherd), which is existence (82–83). He is the novelist in disguise, arriving in the erotic triangle at the end, the god in the machine.

The surface contour of the novel suggests that it is he who gives Rennie the abortion, which is the final mask, which is the gun: "She vomited explosively into the mask. A second later, a horrible sucking sound came from her throat" (181). That it is he who orders Jake back to the "terminal," which is the last immobilization; he whose illegal abortion and, finally, murder caused Joe Morgan to lose his job at Wicomico College, his wife, and his script of values. At another level, it would seem to be Jake, the narrator, the teacher of prescriptive grammar, who pulls all the strings, supplies all the words and the "secret codes" of accidentally accreted grammar, syntax, vocabulary, and meaning which societies agree, masking artifice, to pretend are absolutes of signification (128–29). Jake delights in the game, becomes adept at the masks, but cannot tolerate the gun, the absolute of death. Under Joe and Rennie's pressure, however, he procures this absolute by another means, the oxygen mask of the abortionist. As the arranger of the plot of abortion (both as character and, of course, as narrator) Jake "craves responsibility" at the end, ostensibly seeking a cathartic punishment.

But the codes of the narrator's syntax—" 'Is [the doctor] safe?' Joe asked, a little suspiciously. . . . 'That doesn't matter,' Rennie said quickly" (176)—and of his endgame plot—Joe prepares the fatal dinner, the doctor's examination of Rennie produces no confirmation of her pregnancy—work to throw responsibility back on the husband and wife. Their refusal of a safe abortion under the guise of madness, their refusal to pretend to be anybody but themselves (Jake believes this thickheaded innocence is the ultimate insanity) brings on the desired death.

At midnovel Jake notes that Joe is liable to survive whatever happens, because he "was behaving pretty consistently with his position, and that knowledge can be comforting, even in cases where the position leads to defeat or disaster, when . . . an Othello loves not wisely but too well" (123). Desdemona, like Rennie, had a role played out to the final strangulation: the absolute value of married love. Rennie's pregnancy, like Desdemona's lie about the handkerchief, is simply her contribution to the never-ending story. Barth's abortion, like Shakespeare's murder-suicide, is simply an artist's temporary end, furtively, consolingly, projecting for his culture the death of the woman who, well taught, harbors the single value, the single self. Othello at the end kills the devil Turk who, disguised as himself, killed Desdemona, leaving, we are to believe, the Christian mask alive to continue the marriage during the long journey up the gulfs of fire from purgatory to heaven. At the end of Barth's novel both god and the devil survive, stalemated, irrelevant, with Rennie, the human existent on whom they tested their similar philosophies, gone.

Part of the game of *The End of the Road* was the simultaneous reifying and undermining of the "I," both of personal ego and first person narrative. Part of the game of *Sabbatical* is the attempt to validate, in marriage and in novelistic grammar, a "we" to tell the story. Like the dueling male protagonists of *The End of the Road*, the married man and woman of *Sabbatical* are academics, critics, writers, literately conscious not only, like Joe and Jake in the 1950s, of the secret codes of grammar, but also of post-Derridean accounts of the devious fishtailing of story itself (231). As a fabulist, of course, Barth is elated, not deflated, by this. No Stephen Dedalus, no Joe Morgan or Jake Horner he. Joyce, rather. Homer. God. What makes *Sabbatical* particularly compelling metanarrative is in fact the collision in the style between the kind of "we" he is attempting to create, the truly androgynous storyteller which is the marriage itself ("What we can't do as Fenn and Susan, we can do as Author"[134]), and those ancient, massive models of epic narrative plenitude which parse, finally, as the inflated masculine "I," pushed and pulled, "facilitated," by the feminine muse/auditor.

> There was a story that began,
> Said Fenwick Turner: *Susie and Fenn*—
> Oh, tell that story! tell it again!
> Wept Susan Seckler. (9)

Barth's conceit, conception, in this novel, is that Susan and Fenwick's nine-month's vacationing and stock-taking sabbatical voyage, self-sailed, now ending in the supposedly safe harbor of Chesapeake Bay, represents a story that needs a married telling and a married climax. This suggests to the reader that pregnancy and birth will be the implied plot. Instead we have pregnancy/abortion, an event that the reader is to believe is a mutual, a married one: as it is "our" pregnancy so it is "our" abortion. When birth (rebirth) arrives after all, by a strenuous, a fabulous peripateia, it takes a masculine singular form. The couple's twins disappear forever, sucked out of the salt water of Susan's womb by vacuum aspiration, while Fenn's lucky Basque hat, affectionately lamented as "mi boina" throughout, returns from the Bay into which it disappeared in the first chapter.

The married lovers of the story have taken this sabbatical—she in the regular teaching cycle; he after publishing an exposé of, and detaching himself from, his activities in the CIA; "we" after the magic first seven years of good luck in a marriage have passed, and certain strains and questions are emerging—in order to clarify and make choices on each individual, and on the mutual marriage, level.

Fenn is a fifty-year-old man with a grown son from an earlier marriage and a thirty-year, on and off affair with both the muse of story—frustrating, often impotent and "unreal" but relatively harmless copulation—and the muse of history, political engagement—a potent but ultimately death-dealing one. His "worldly twin," (31) Manfred, the Mephistopheles of this novel, drew him into his own bailiwick, the CIA, when as a young, unsuccessful novelist Fenn "decided to live a story, since I couldn't write one," wishing to "operate on history instead of being operated on by It" (44). This decision drew him into the CIA's covert actions during the 1970s, into Iran, Vietnam, Chile, hoping to "do white stuff to counteract or compensate for [his twin's] black stuff" (181). In the late 1970s Fenn withdrew from history, appalled, with a story instead, a published exposé of CIA covert actions which left him sufficiently personna non grata with his former colleagues to raise the question whether a recent, massive heart attack might have been "induced" by something from the Company's secret arsenal of biochemical weapons. Whether that "episode" is part of a CIA "story" or the natural history of his body, a kind of endgame clock has been set ticking in his life. His sabbatical is to decide what kind of writing or teaching to do now and to decide what the recent disappearance of his worldly twin off a boat in Chesapeake Bay, and the "disappearing" of Manfred's rebellious son, Gus, by the Chilean police, should mean for his relationship to story and to history.

For thirty-five-year-old Susan Seckler clocks are ticking, too. A gifted teacher and fledgling scholar in a community college, it is time for her to make a move, if she is going to, to the more taxing but, in a certain sense, less "real" world of high-powered literary scholarship and first-class universities. Childless by choice after seven years of marriage, she needs to confirm or reverse that choice, while she has a choice.

Once again the pregnancy seems a gun aimed at someone. This is true in the first chapter, where pregnant Susan lays her ear against Fenn's chest and feels her heart break to hear his damaged heart beat, and he lays his ear to her belly in ambiguous search (is it really there? is it still there?) for the heartbeat in her womb (26). One of the two hearts, it seems, is going to, will be forced to, "go off." The choice is made in the last chapter of the novel when Susan, now fallen from the ideal "we" of her marriage to the enforced solitude, as it must be, of this life-and-death choice, tersely explains her decision to her doctor:

> I faked my last two periods, but I know Fenn knows we're pregnant. He'd rather not raise another child, but he wishes I had one. I didn't tell him I was pregnant because I didn't want to tell him I was going to abort because I didn't want to upset him; I was afraid he'd have another heart attack. I think it's really strange not to have children, but it's my decision, and my considered decision is Abort. All right? (291)

Affirming "you're the doctor," Morris Steinfeld performs the clean and tidy, painless procedure: "It is the little fetus, she supposes, that succumbs to two particularly nasty almost feral schlups from the machine, which subsequently purrs like a fed cat. 'Some women,' Morris says, injecting a little medical humor, 'aspire to motherhood. Others have lower aspirations' " (295).

The narrative organizes the pregnancy and the gun (the heart attack) together as potential destroyers of the marriage. Fenn and Susan, who have throughout, in dialogues of opinions and in exchanges of stories, created the "we" of marriage and narrative, who have created "our" pregnancy, withhold from each other two crucial stories: he of a second heart attack, she of the pregnancy and abortion. Though these don't happen chronologically together, the narrative's rhetoric steadily links them—"Subdued Fenwick decides not to tell her now. Subdued Susan decides not to tell him now" (243)—with each other. And with the gun. Musing on the second episode of heart failure and the possibility of its CIA instigation, Fenn recognizes the harbinger of his death merely as a harbinger, answering no to the storyteller's question, "Can a pistol hung on the wall in Act One . . . be fired in Act One?" (152).

In act three, on Friday the thirteenth, Black Friday, Fenn goes to the funeral of the friend he had speculated might have given him the heart-attack-triggering poison, himself now mysteriously dead of a heart attack, and receives another pitch from the Prince of Darkness's world to be a double agent. And Susan goes to Morris Steinfeld. The pistol fired in this act hits the pregnancy and now can be returned to the closet of history where the CIA and the Defense Department go their destroying way, or of nature where the heart of the fifty-year-old male and the ovaries of the thirty-five-year-old woman shrink in anticipation of the end. In a terrible, mutual, precognitive dream the night before Black Friday, "one of us has brute flashes of apocalypse: the thunderous destruction of great cities by men who have never seen them; to whom Leningrad, Firenze, San Francisco are mere target-names. The other of us dreams of the one's death and of sick old age in a nursing home without the care and comfort of children, grandchildren." Racked by incipient loss, they wake "to an ugly sucking noise" (a dog slurps his food outside their bedroom door) "and reach for one another" (286). And this, for man the bearer of history, woman the bearer of children, is "our" abortion.

It is no accident that the history, the pregnancy, aborted here, was twins. The "worldly twin" who entered history, the twins who express "world" in reality, represent for Barth that principle of paired opposition first depicted in the two snakes that paralyze and strangle Laocoon in the sculpture on the mantelpiece in the room rented by the earlier novel's Jake Horner. Twins connote the hopeless deadlock—mutual attraction, mutual opposition—of "reality." Nothing but a "magical" meeting of these twins, egg and sperm, will bring to birth a living wholeness.[5]

The dreamed destruction of the real, nonmagical twins is a rhetorical moment of great power, sexual stereotypes notwithstanding. Yet in Barth sexual stereotypes are not really withstood. When Barth is creating "the ballast of realism" (137) for his pregnant woman protagonist in *Sabbatical*, he equips her with an updated version of the no exit psychoanalytic situation of Joe Morgan. For Joe, marriage was the ultimate, if artificial and willed, value, so ultimate that it was impossible to fulfill. And for Susan, parenthood is so profound a value that she fears it as much as she craves it: "being an ordinary mediocre parent doesn't interest me. . . . my standards for it are self-defeatingly high. . . . I'd fail myself and my children . . . even a terrific child, which is the only kind I want" (164). Fenn's son was conceived by an accident, an inadequate condom. Barth reprises the burst condom-brings-pregnancy story of *The End of the Road* twice in *Sabbatical:* once when Susan and Fenn first make landfall on an uncharted island in Chesapeake Bay, and they find a burst condom and an empty beer bottle: "Aha, says Fenwick: there's a story there. Susan murmurs poor girl. Not a new story, though" (49); and again in the flashback to Fenn's first marriage:

> But in the early Nineteen Fifties it is no joke when a condom fails, and Marilyn Marsh discovers herself in the family way—almost if not quite certainly by Fenn. [His Prince of Darkness twin had also slept with Marilyn.] Strictly raised, she's in a panic. I'd've been too. Knowledgeable Count [the twin] proposes abortion and quickly makes the illegal arrangements. Innocent Fenn proposes marriage and is accepted. (175)

But knowledge and innocence are no longer separable twins; neither are choice and accident. The unplanned pregnancy that is the concern of the novel partakes of both. After the abortion Susan says wryly: "We made do with a diaphragm, but we weren't as careful as we should have been. Maybe we wanted it to happen so we'd know for sure what we felt. I hate psychology" (292).

Susan may have wished that Fenn's male desire to propagate another child would sweep away her own apprehensions, reservations, and choices about parenthood, but his desire has taken a turn new to her, though common in Barth's work. For Fenn is incubating another offspring—the story. There is, he says, using an old euphemism for pregnancy, "that novel in the oven, or play, or whatever" (149). The one "we" are now writing. And of course, reading. It's called *Sabbatical,* but the fathering text is Shakespeare's *The Tempest,* being reread (and, of course, rewritten) "for the hundredth time" (201) by the two people on board. The novel may be a realistic story about burst condoms, lower aspirations, and the woe of human choicemaking and human limitations. But the fable, "the play or whatever," is pure Shakespeare, benignly patriarchal. In it, "Graybeard Fenn . . . grizzled Fenwick" (9), the Prospero of all the novel's island kingdoms, step-uncle and lover, if not father, of the fertile Susan, his Miranda, takes up the magic of storytelling in which conception, *the* conception, is sundered from sex, leaving the two activities to go their enjoyably parallel but not congruent ways.[6]

The novel's ending is a sea of fantasy blending the best of Shakespeare with the worst of Mailer. Fenn's imagination has been "fertilised" (330) by an idea from Susan's mother, that a man's or a woman's "real" children are not the ones conceived in sexual congress but rather the ova and the sperm produced in solitude, monthly in her case, irregularly in his, and shed "down the pipes" (127) into the world's seas. There, very rarely, a fated sperm and egg may meet and join, not briefly, as in human copulation, but "literally and for keeps," like the lost halves imagined in Plato's Symposium. And these unitary wholes, nonhuman parents if somewhat like their human sources, may in time generate, asexually, their like, something terrible and wonderful, a marvel (241–42).

This Marvel rises out of the Bay in the final pages, a sea monster, huge, smooth, powerful, unconcerned, featureless but for an eye, "round, bright, black and perfectly expressionless" (342). So much has gone into the sea in this story: Fenn's worldly twin, Susan's aborted twins, Fenn's lucky "boina," the ex-operative John Arthur Paisley (a paisley print looks like scores of sperm, Fenn notes unnecessarily often for his fable). What has come back, transformed by sea change? Those are pearls that were his eyes. Not children. "We" will be childless. Not the worldly twin: "we" will be *in* the world, take jobs, pursue careers, but not *of* it, nothing from that world "has us really by the throat" (360). After the sighting of the sea monster (Chessie, is it? The camera can't tell.) Susan surprises Fenn, herself, and the reader, surely, by telling him she thinks he has got it in him to be a real artist, not just a good writer. "That sea monster was important," Fenn exults; "There's a power I didn't know about, and now I think I've got it. Maybe I had it all along; that doesn't matter. You gave it to me by naming it. In fact, it's not mine, but ours" (351).

So. This is not a new story either, is it? Barth's influential 1967 essay on the "Literature of Exhaustion" suggested two meanings for this term, and the iconography of pregnancy—*male* pregnancy—fits both.[7] The mid-twentieth-century (male) writer, exhausted by the achievements of his predecessors, can bring nothing original to birth and must find a way to say this—"Terminal." The (male) writer, fathering not one but a thousand and one stories, must create and exhaust all of them, countering real exhaustion with "magical" infinity, father/mothering myth. Portrait of the artist as a sea monster, a sperm swimming "steadily but unhurriedly northward like a giant tadpole toward Love Point Light and the open Bay" (342). Out to forge the uncreated conscience of his race in the smithy of his soul. Pardon me, "our" soul. "Our story, it's our house and child" (357), Fenwick declares to Susan, whose heart obligingly "fills, less unequivocally but no less lovingly than his" (363). She is, "given the magnitude of her love" (363), willing to substitute learning and civilization, story, for parenthood. The final image of "us"—disturbing amalgam of Homer, Shakespeare, and, Barth's all-time favorite muse, Scheherazade—offers a patriarch's image of the adult male artist feeding from his daughter/mother:

"Years ago, on our first visit as lovers to this island, she might have felt as excited and unsure as young Nausica might have, had she eloped with briny, middle-aged Odysseus. Now, as his familiar hand takes her breast, she feels like a confident Scheherazade, hundreds of nights after that first, upon the lap of her long-since-conquered king" (263).

Margaret Drabble: The Child Inside

Margaret Drabble's heroines are always "good" girls—responsible, hard-working, independent women following plans, committed to reason, though troubled with the inherited conscience of the nonconforming middle classes. Her novels are "realistic," which means not only that they abound in the concrete details of ordinary life—the contents of purses, of sewers, of postboxes and newspapers—not only that the shaping hands of class, education, money, age, history, and memory are primary, but also that the shaping hand of the storyteller, really primary, is hidden in the elaborately recreated randomness, disorder, of the apparently plotless reality of daily living. The disorder itself, often benignly comic, located in "lists" and the "scraps, orts and fragments" of a Virginia Woolfian sensibility, has yet its darker, Hardyesque fatality as well.[8] The "good" girl with her order, reality with its disorder, collide in these two novels in the ancient icon of the pregnant woman, hugely weighted, a marvel, a kind of land monster.

In the 1965 novel, *The Millstone,* a pregnant woman with two small children toils painfully down the road. Finally, brought to a standstill waiting for the dawdling two-year-old, "eyes fixed," the one-year-old "slung, legs astride, over the swelling of the next. . . . She stood there, patiently waiting, like a warning, like a portent, like a figure from another world."[9] In the 1980 novel, *The Middle Ground,* the forty-year-old protagonist pauses in a room in the National Gallery featuring paintings of women setting out on journeys: "Embarkation. Her heart stirred." She turns then to an antithetical ideograph: "Psyche Locked Out of the Palace of Cupid," of "The Enchanted Castle." Psyche, "heavy, dull, large-limbed, dark, a large woman clearly abandoned," swelled and petrified with the fruits of her loving, sits seeking entrance, and Kate Fletcher Armstrong apostrophizes her and herself: "And there beyond them, again, the sea, and little white sails free in the wind, in the sunlight. Why did not Psyche look up and see all that glittering expanse? . . . She should look up, and move, and go. The castle of love was a prison, a fortress, a tomb, how could she not appreciate her luck in being locked out?"[10]

Ancient, dark weight, the burden of loving paralyzes woman. Yet for anyone who harms children, it has been declared, it were better to be thrown into the sea with a millstone tied round her neck (Matthew 18 : 6). And the millstone grinds corn. For the protagonist of the earlier novel her disciplined and enjoyable work as a literary scholar, her active but sexless social life, her healthy, self-reliant freedom, are her choice, her reward, her delight, even her nature, and, in the watches of the night, at the prodding of her conscience, "my poverty" (49). When the millstone of love comes with its huge and potentially permanent weight of pregnancy, some preternatural force inclines her beyond the logic of abortion and the poverty of freedom toward the dark riches of slavery—motherhood.

The Millstone, like Barth's novels, essays a comic tone with some dark undertones: as with Barth the main characters are writers, self-consciously offering parallels about the two kinds of conception. (Drabble was in her third pregnancy while writing this her third novel.) Rosamond Stacey is finishing her doctoral thesis like Joe Morgan: she even "amused myself by trying to finish my thesis before my baby, matching will against destiny," though will "flags" as destiny begins to require the mind's energy along with the body's to complete the pregnancy (100). Rosamond's friend, Lydia, a novelist stuck for a story, moves in with her and writes, secretly, the story of Rosamond's choice as she imagines it for her character, her friend— a choice that involves the ancient assumption that birth will validate the woman's love for the child's father, activate his toward her, and result in a normal, married, familial triangle. Lydia once lived out the approved novelist's fiction on this point. Heavy with unloving, illegitimate pregnancy, Lydia shrank from that catch-22 of the 1960s whereby a woman had to be declared mentally unstable for a legal abortion, though an abortion would so traumatize an unstable woman that it could not be recommended by the doctor. But chance took care of the solution: walking away from the doctor's office she fell in front of a bus and miscarried. Rejecting that (true) plot as too novelistic and too self-exposing, Lydia writes up what she imagined Rosamond's truth was, "racking her brain trying to work out why I was having the child, and why I didn't get rid of it" (104).

Rosamond finishes the pregnancy and the thesis as well. Lydia's novel gets hit by a bus and miscarries: that is, Rosamond's baby, crawling and curious, finds Lydia's, not her mother's, manuscript and chews up, tears up, or otherwise destroys all but pages 70–123. Lydia, surprisingly calm, rewrites it, changing it in unspecified ways and gets her first bad reviews when it is published.

The protagonist of Lydia's novel, the "me-character" as Rosamond calls her, uses academic scholarship as an escape from the disorderly realities of personality and relationship. She decides for birth as another kind of escape: her "jigsaw mind" seeks the child as the piece that will make an orderly triangle of woman, child, and lover.

Rosamond's actual motives are linked with these, but far stranger. Her nature, which is chaste, self-reliant, and self-making, bars her, she believes, from the two situations her culture associates with "reality"—love and suffering. She studies these situations in her chosen critical field, the sixteenth-century English sonnet. She circles round them in a life lived rather like a restoration comedy, concealing the "crime" of virginity (20), the "poverty" (49) of her abstinence, under an elaborate dual "affair" in which each man thinks she is sleeping with the other. Her culture, her parents, even her conscience think she should be interested not in these stylized forms of poetry but in the "life-bearing" precincts, as F. R. Leavis would have it, of the nineteenth-century novel. That same conscience reproaches her that her "crime" was not "the good old traditional one of lust and greed" but rather "a brand-new twentieth-century crime . . . my suspicion, my fear, my apprehensive terror of the very idea of sex" (21). Like her sixteenth-century sonneteers, Rosamond likes being "in love," but "making love" confers that millstone, opens that enchanted castle which is also a prison.

She doesn't want it, doesn't need it, the poetry could not survive with it.

And yet, of course, the "story" needs it, the novel needs it. Drabble provides it in a brief encounter of considerable comic pathos between George, an "unassertive" and "feminine" acquaintance whom Rosamond thinks is safely homosexual, and the heroine, who has unstintingly given George the impression she is intelligently promiscuous. Cool and friendly and armored in their modern determination not to bring pressures, not to make assumptions, not to be millstones, George and Rosamond talk a bit, listen to the radio, drift toward each other, mutely signal permissions. Rosamond adjusts her mental state: she likes him alright, and besides, "it would be good for me. . . . And then that was it and it was over" (34–35).

To her shock, "making love" delivered just what she had feared it would. Even with George what came was love, suffering, change, "reality." Not in the approved novelistic way, however. Both she and George, the narrative hints, had experienced the ambiguous desire that makes love suffering, the desire to totally possess just that one beloved thing out of all the world's objects. In this scene early in the book and in the one other meeting that closes the book, each seems "on the verge of some confession, some confidence, some approach that once made could never be denied," that once made would do the "damage" that love does (188–89). But neither makes that approach in either scene, so practiced is each at that modern self-reliance which ends in indifference. They are the same person, the same modern nature, and their fate would have been the same, quiet not unfruitful immersion in that prized modern kingdom, "a life of my own" (187), except for the "accident," the "choice" of womanhood in Rosamond's case, which provides in the form of a pregnancy, not a lover but the millstone of reality.

Self-reliance inclined Rosamond to self-induced abortion when this millstone first appeared: a dimly remembered prescription from cheap fiction, gin and hot baths, doesn't "take." Self-reliance dictates, in a bitter aftermath, that she personally "pay" for her womanhood with a pregnancy. Self-reliance boasts, in an early debate with her married, childed sister over adoption, that she is not only equal to single, illegitimate parenthood but potentially a better mother than any adoptive parent in England. Simultaneously, being pregnant opens up the aspects of life her nature couldn't choose, had given her no access to, but which her conscience did choose—dependency, ignorance, suffering, confinement, invasion. Rosamond's choosing nature and her importuning conscience opt for a maternal choice of birth intellectually as an "initiation into reality" (41), an entrance onto another "nonrational" plane of meaning which is, paradoxically, though it means "learning to live within a human limit" (65), also an extension of the self, an enlargement. As a student, a teacher, a writer, Rosamond thinks in these terms, rationalizing the irrational, controlling "reality" by naming it. Pregnancy is a state of enforced changes, wearying, invasive, yet for the trained, critical mind it is all a familiar process of discovery—so familiar that this access to the plane of irrational forces, the "camp of intuition" (76), actually increases her power to do her work on the sixteenth-century sonneteers until the very last minute.

The great change comes with birth, a profound, inner revolution beyond intellectual anticipation. The moment of birth is rhetorically linked to the mute moment of conception—George then and Rosamond now say it's "pointless" to describe their feelings. Rosamond is kept awake both times by the unfamiliar and much guarded against sensation of "happiness" (34–35, 114–15). The revolution happens here simply because while modern adults may be too diffident or thoughtful or guarded to bring pressure, make approaches, form millstones, babies are not. With adults, "if one of us did not move towards the other, then we could only move apart" (187), but a newborn baby always makes the first move and so unlocks love in the adult. Rosamond's daughter greets her immediately, Rosamond imagines, not only with "recognition" but also with "such wreathing, dazzling gaiety of affection" that it "left me free to bestow love" (114, 128). As with the sonneteer, it is her own power to love which concerns Rosamond: little Octavia "had no option" but to love her (128) and neither, loosed from the paralyzing modern constraints of free will, had Rosamond. Liberated precariously into the two camps of reason and unreason, elated with her own absurdity, "I don't believe in principle," says Rosamond, "I believe in instinct, on principle" (127).

Now "quite unmistakeably up against no choice" (129), Rosamond is stirred by the appalling discovery that a mother is a being in need, must rely on others for help, from doctors and druggists to baby-sitters and the most casual passersby. She also discovers that just as the baby's dependency unlocked her love, her dependency unlocks other people's kind response: "If I asked more favours of people, I would find people more kind" (179). Even the Deity is un-covered/created in this process. Octavia has a serious, if invisible, birth defect, a flawed heart, apparently, which requires a life-threatening operation to correct. The night before the operation finds Rosamond in true nonconformist rage and arrogance searching her own life for the "crime" of which Octavia's suffering is the retribution. She comes close to naming her sin, when, mistakenly naming it "my love for her," she "almost hoped that she might die; and thus relieve me of the corruption and fatality of love" (141). More simply, in dire distress, she "got down on my knees and said, Oh God, let her survive, let her live, let her be alright, and God was created by my need, perhaps" (141).

The novel's resolution, enigmatic, triumphant but disturbing, occurs as Octavia survives the operation but hospital rules forbid mothers visiting infant children. Up to this time, trouble, opposition, had been something to be arranged in the head between self and self, to be endured or ignored by the strong minded. Now, with a sick, lonely child lying terrified in bandages in a bed behind several locked doors, action in the world, corrupt, fatal, and selfish, is required: "It was no longer a question of what I wanted: this time there was someone else involved. Life would never be a simple question of self-denial again" (147).

Rosamond stands firm against hospital middle management—all women—fighting the rules of order, of fairness, of good sense, until a shrieking, Amazonian harpy is liberated in her. The triumph is that this impassioned madwoman and the reasoning, intellectual scholar find coexistence, not mutual hostility: "I remember also the clearness of my consciousness, and the ferocity of my emotion, and myself enduring them, myself neither one nor the other, but enduring them and not breaking in two" (149). Not breaking in two, now a stable "I," neither the self-denying child of her parents nor the maternal fury but someone who can use each where necessary, Rosamond feels a new "sense of adequacy. I knew something now of the quality of life" (158). By the end of the novel she is contemplating with irony the "growing selfishness" which is "probably maturity" (161).

More enigmatic and disturbing undercurrents in this quality of life, however, than the paradoxical selfishness which replaces intellectualized and self-protecting self-denial, are two other discoveries in this scene. In the hospital battle Rosamond won visitation rights over the "sister" who managed the floor because of the influence of her male doctor, a friend of her father's. Another successfully visiting mother won her battle because her husband was an important man: "I don't know what one would do without a little influence" (153). The quality of this life is that mothers can mother only through the influence of men.

On the other hand, though Rosamond meets George again at the novel's end and feels again that "gaiety" which signals the approach of love, another love, *the* love "had isolated me more securely than fear, habit, or indifference" (191). The "faint, constant and pearly" light of maternal love, "a bad investment . . . one that would leave me in the dark and the cold in years to come," has wiped out the "perplexed fitful illuminations" of heterosexual love (191). She has "spared" George the "sorrow" but also, of course, the potential knowledge of the quality of life that might have been his with the knowledge of his paternity. The novel is unclear whether she does this out of compassion or parsimony, out of the rigidity of old habits of self-reliance, or because the "complete knowledge" of the child, which both activates and isolates her in her loving, can only be experienced by the female parent.[11] The last, it would seem, from the bleak but obliquely complementary close of the novel.

"I can't help worrying," I said. "It's my nature. There's nothing I can do about my nature, is there?"

"No," said George, his hand upon the door. "No, nothing." (192)[12]

Indeed, the limiting of loving, for this woman at least, purely to the maternal is rhetorically expressed as a birth of maternity and an abortion of adult heterosexuality: "It was *no longer in me*" to love in both ways, says Rosamond (my italics, 191).

The question—what is woman's nature, and how large or ambiguously damaging a part of it is "the maternal instinct"—dominates *The Middle Ground,* another novel whose fulcrum is pregnancy and the choice to bear or abort the millstone which both drowns and gives corn, life, purpose. Once again the inconvenient and "illegitimate" pregnancy comes at first with the sweet force of a divine "visitation" (59), a meaning giver. Once again, suggestively, the fetus is genetically flawed. This time, ambiguous blessing of 1980s technology, the mother knows that in the first trimester. This time the thirty-nine-year-old Kate Armstrong, divorced mother of three children, had aborted a fourth child just before the novel opens. And she wrestles with the aftermath throughout, seeking to know whether the act had outraged or confirmed her "nature": "A healthy person conceiving a sick child. Impossible, impossible, she could not accept such knowledge. She had cut out the child, but not the malady" (101–2).

Kate's midlife search for her nature, her womanhood, is complicated, as was Rosamond's, by certain twentieth-century twists on the old problems. The sexual revolution that had made virginity, not promiscuity, the "crime" in Rosamond's 1960s generation, has now, in the hyperconscious feminist eighties, made marriage seem the warping trap, careers the sanctuary of freedom, independent selfhood the socially approved norm, and motherhood, mothering, a devious form of manipulation and a running out on one's own inner growth. A member of "the revolution" early as a journalist and columnist on women's issues in the seventies, Kate has at thirty-nine become lost in the ideological debates she herself has helped initiate and conduct. She is "haunted" by warring concepts of the "real Woman" (166). One concept, admittedly supportive of, perhaps even invented by, patriarchy, is centered on female "loving" and confirmed by maternity; the other concept, a feminist-heroic ideal modeled on the quest pattern, is always seeking growth, new challenges, "embarkation," in the iconography of the novel. And she's losing faith or interest in this latter womanhood, Kate complains half humorously, half despairingly to her friend and cousin, Hugo Mainwaring, partly because she helped originate it: "I'm sick to death of [women], I wish I'd never invented them" (2).

The irony is, as flashbacks to Kate's adolescence and early womanhood make clear, that Kate first invented herself as feminist questor only partly in class rebellion against lower middle-class Romley where she grew up, in emotional rebellion against a rationalist, sewer worker father and a withdrawn, housebound mother. She also reinvented herself in an oblique kind of emulation of the implied narratives of womanly success imposed on her in television ads and "downscale" women's magazines of the late 1950s, those about which Betty Friedan later wrote *The Feminine Mystique:*

> Something in her was entranced by the gap between fantasy and reality. The happy endings to the stories of those who found love because they had learned about BO in time, who became ballerinas because they discovered hand cream (yes, hand cream), who were promoted to manageress status because they started to drink Horlick's, filled her with a profound and mysterious satisfaction. (22)

Moving towards that better life, intelligently suspicious though entranced, the child Kate remade herself from a profane, fighting little street arab who secretly loved fairy tales into a witty class clown who dominated her teenage friends by making them laugh and by leading them in audacious "confessions" about the problems of their advancing puberty. These teenage qualities were the materials for the bold, young newspaper columnist she became in her twenties, who broke new ground in writing openly about women's lives. Her early success came because her copy on womanhood contained elements of both "parody and sincerity" (30); she consolidated her position as spokeswoman for a self-conscious generation of new women by writing about forbidden topics "before they became fashionable, sharing her pregnancies and exhaustions and indignations with a shocked and enthralled public" (32).

"Unashamedly a woman's writer" (32), hard-working Kate acquired everything the magazine narratives promised: love, a husband, children, success. She did it not by using hand cream but using the other tools of middle-class life—ambition, witty banter, fictions of control—that moved her away from her origins even more effectively. In the 1970s feminism changed the pattern, if only slightly, and Kate, setting and following the pattern in parody and sincerity, divorced her inept, artist-husband, Stuart, and acquired a handsome and brilliant scientist-lover, Ted, whose long-time, not-to-be-renounced marriage to Evelyn makes Kate's new womanhood perfect. She has love, career, grown, problem free children, and freedom.

At age thirty-nine, right on cue, the year before the novel opens, midlife crisis strikes: all its forms connote the return, the revenge, of motherhood and dependency. She becomes "professionally restless." The fighting feminism she has been working with successfully for so long produces a novel (Marilyn French's *The Women's Room*) which she feels reduces life with children to an unfair and unreal sequence of "shit and string beans." The maternal instinct, recoiling with "unease and distaste" as much from the novel's bestsellerdom as from its image, alienates her from feminism (53) and from the newspaper she wrote feminist columns for. She reads some contemporary studies about probable, negative side effects of the birth control pill for the older woman and another radical feminist indictment of the pill as a "male weapon designed to sterilize womanhood" (57–58) and goes off the pill, forgetting to tell her moody and desperate lover (he has in fact tired of Kate and taken a new mistress but can't tell her).

The pregnancy which results (Drabble's Victorian storytelling hand is nowhere so evident as in these catastrophic, one encounter pregnancies, as her narrator admits in *The Millstone*) shatters the affair with Ted, exposing her to herself, a person she doesn't know and doesn't much like.

> She did not tell Ted. . . . She feared either his acceptance or rejection. There was no room for him in her house or in her life, on anything other than a part-time basis. But she did not like the knowledge that he might feel the same about her. So what had she been playing at? Not love, surely. Maybe she had never loved anybody, except her children.

But if she loved her children (which she did not doubt),
why not have another one and extend her years of loving?
(60)

Yet "loving" in the mode of motherhood has itself become suspect
to Kate: this mode in which the woman stays "on top," ever self-
reliant, apparently drowned in the claims of the dependent, apparently caught in the undertow of her nature's "steady pull toward
the lost" (218)—puppy, kitten, pigeon, stray child of any age or
sex—unable to say no. But at bottom, she recognizes "saying yes
is . . . my way of keeping the upper hand" (8).

Is it "feminism" that has poisoned that natural maternal yea saying with its artificial, ideological suspicions? Or has Kate's rejection
of her lower middle-class girlhood and her nonmothering mother
addicted her early to that female kind of "leadership" which is the
influencing of superiors, the secret transformation of others into de-
pendents? "I like everyone to depend on me, whyever is that?"
Kate frets (8). And again: "She asked herself this constant-
ly . . . was her thwarted maternal instinct misdirecting her, making
her treat men as children who wouldn't be able to survive without
her care? Did she *wish* to so regard them? . . . Did she connive at
their folly? Well, yes, she did. But *why*?" (69).

Or is there perhaps a world historical, a colonialist-imperialist as-
pect, to the sudden discovery that an ancient, formerly acceptable,
pattern of purposeful dependency is poisoned? The "caring professions," western civilization's pride, the dream achievement of the
1960s, are in the eighties in England "plunging into a dark swamp
of uncertainty, self-questioning, economic crisis" (54). Kate's social
worker friend, Evelyn, toiling on in good conscience at the so-
ciological equivalent of maternity with her clients, can't confess
even to this best friend the secret, "frightening visions" she has of
herself "attacking" her frail and elderly welfare "children" (56).
Kate's radical Arab houseguest, another of the "lost" that her
nature can't say no to, would analyze it this way, Kate thinks. He
would say that capitalism's "ethic of care" is a secret way of producing client nations, client races: "This is the disease of capitalism. The
final sickness. . . . And would he be right? God knows, for I cer-

tainly don't. Oh, Lord, thought Kate, first I had a Freudian nervous breakdown through Ted and that baby business, and now I'm having a Marxist nervous breakdown through Mujid" (99).

Part of Kate's "nervous breakdown" comes from the middle-aged person's simple and, up to a point, healthy loss of grip on, belief in, the "patterns and programmes" (213) which as a young person s/he selected out as "the truth" about her/his nature, or the nature of the age. Pushed too far, this loss of belief results in a cynical, world nausea where every value is dismissed as "pretense," and every choice damned as giving merely the illusion of progress. Kate approaches this dangerous state of paralysis, akin to Barth's "terminal" state of scriptlessness, as pregnancy is discovered, and the fetus's flaw is diagnosed as spina bifida. The temptation to be a mother even to so damaged a baby is strong: "She would be a woman again" (63). Suffering with that suffering child, she might even become a kind of saint, anchored in faith, in unreasoning instinct: "Never again would she have to contemplate the blank waste of freedom" (64).

Finally Kate does have the abortion and, plunging fully into the blank waste, undergoes sterilization as well. The picture of herself as the suffering mother, hugging the millstone, seems a "wicked temptation," a destructive masque to involve herself, her children, her friends in: "She had no right to invoke suffering. So she argued, and knew that she was right. But it was not easy to choose the right thing. She suffered" (64).

"Choosing the right thing," acting intelligently against the maternal undertow, means for Kate a nightmare year of breakdowns. At night motherhood strikes back in bad dreams of dead babies, pigeons, dogs; in the daylight Kate struggles to say yes to the lost and needy in a rational, compassionate, and productive manner, not in the obsessed, secretly manipulative way she feared had become her habit, if not her "nature".

> "This," she says, "is the Armageddon—or do I mean Waterloo?—of the maternal instinct": She watches its thrashing and struggling with an amazed and sad detachment. "What is it for?" (79)

The maternal instinct in its most material, irrational form, spine-damaged like the fetus, must be abandoned, and the instinct itself transformed. The symbolic force of Kate's early question—can a healthy woman (maternal instinct) conceive a sick child?—locates the sickness in Kate's overripe, secretly tyrannical maternalizing. The choice is to "cut it out"; the nightmares, the blank waste of freedom, are part of the cost.

The realistic novelist gives no direct answers to the questions that plague her protagonist: How does one make choices after patterns and programmes, ideologies and isms have lost their status as absolutes? How can we tell, devious egoists that we are, whether we ever have "truly loved," or can love? And, most vexing of all, what is the maternal instinct *for,* after "the time for children is over [and] it is time for the next thing, whatever it may be?"[13] But the fabulist within the realistic novelist has offered a hint in the last third of the novel as Kate goes back to Romley to research a TV documentary on today's women making choices and, of course, to recover her own origins as well.

Still troubled by the abortion and its violation of her motherhood/womanhood, she rereads a Russian fairy tale she once loved as a child—a tale of a young sister who sacrificed herself for a careless brother and was drowned but resurrected. The tale has some resonance for the brother and sister, Peter and Kate, of long-ago Romley, who lost each other as Kate fought her way to self-reliance and middle-class, feminist gentility. But the real resurrection in this and the other fairy tales Kate reads has to do with an inner, lost self, one associated with the chosen abortion: "In the story she comes to life again," Kate muses, "but in real life, no doubt, she stayed dead" (192). The resurrection is that of the child she once was, who loved her profane, street friends and her paranoid, sewer worker father and her idle, agoraphobic mother before she "learned" there was something "wrong" with that life. Kate suspects that the real abortion happened back then.

Those two selves, that prattling, chattering journalist in Kentish Town, with her smart views and expensive boots and trendy house, and the child in its skimpy cotton dress, lonely, cast out, cut off—what had they in common? No blood flowed from one to the other, the cord was cut, she withered and grew dry. (109)

The "smart view" is that the growing adult must reject the child inside, as the actual child must reject the parent; "that it was dangerous, destructive, to try to preserve communion, to try to keep the blood flowing through the severed chord" (112). But the fable clearly takes the opposite view that what the maternal instinct is *for* is to keep the blood flowing through the cord. The time for children is never over until the child self, however flawed, split, is resurrected; "the next thing" cannot even be glimpsed until the child within is cared for like the child outside. This done, the fable hopes, the re-animation of love in all directions is possible.

The Middle Ground, true to the form of its realism, ends, or rather, arbitrarily halts, with Kate perplexed in the midst of choices again—the low mimetic ones (which inadequate dress will she wear to her party?) and the high mimetic ones (which "embarkation" comes next? a new career? a new lover?) which make up the spontaneous, patternless progress of a real life. But the fable climaxes in a beautiful vision, embodying a Dickensian certainty bracketed resolutely with Drabble's own twentieth-century question marks, of restoration, connection, blood flowing through all the secretly connected cords.

From the twelfth-floor window, London stretched away, St. Paul's in the distance, and the towers of the City, and beneath them, nearby, the little network of streets, back yards, cul-de-sacs, canals, warehouses, curves and chimneys, railways, little factories tucked into odd corners; unplanned, higgledy-piggledy, hardly a corner wasted, intricate, enmeshed, patched and pieced together, the old and the new side by side, overlapping, jumbled, always decaying yet always renewed; London, how could one ever be tired of it? How could one stumble dully through its streets, or waste time sitting in a heap staring at a wall? When there it lay, its old intensity restored, shining with in-

vitation, all its shabby grime lost in perspective, impercepti-
ble from this dizzy height, its connections clear, its path-
ways revealed. The city, the kingdom. The aerial view. Kate
gazed east towards Romley. The little sister is resurrected,
dug up, dragged from the river, the stone that weighted her
dissolves, she rises up. Perhaps, perhaps, thought Kate, and
turned back to Evelyn, who was sitting up, her arms
around her knees, looking like a child in her striped night-
dress, a child except for her greying hair. The aerial view of
human love, where all connections are made known,
where all roads connect? (225–26)

*

In the story she comes to life again: in real life, no doubt, she
stayed dead." To paraphrase the keynote of my introduction,
plots about abortion may begin with reasons and proceed to
choices, but they always rely on story to bring back the dead, to
undo the mortal and fatal choices that mark real life and restore the
plurality, the simultaneity, which characterize desire, especially maternal desire. Indeed, whether pregnancy, potentiality, results in
abortion or birth, a lost motherhood or a found one, a child self resurrected from memory or one embodied in a new life, the mortal
fact of real life is contained in Rosamond's elegy, "it was no longer in
me." "It" is either lost (Rennie's being) or split, fictionalized "outside me" (Susan's motherhood, Rosamond's "love," Kate's little
sister/self). Life whole, a network of connections known yet "unplanned . . . intricate, enmeshed," the "oceanic" of the psychol-
ogists, the "aerial view" of the fabulists: this is the lost territory of
the undelivered, maternal body, site both of the abortion plot (every
choice enacts some abortion) and of the yearning "perhaps, perhaps" that tries to undo that plot.

2
"We Are Not Dying":
Abortion and Recovery in
Four Novels by Women

The decade which saw the institutionalization of the right not to become a mother saw many women writers affirming daughterhood more powerfully than ever. If, as George Eliot says, every limit is a beginning as well as an ending, so also the response to a removal of limits may be an instinctive grasp at an anchor—mother, or motherhood.

In Joan Didion's *Play It as It Lays* (1970) and Margaret Atwood's *Surfacing* (1972), the abortion on which the plot hinges is an encounter with nonbeing, which threatens the extinction of female personality. The plot conflates the imaginary recovery of the lost child with the recovery of the mother and of the self. In Didion's existential romance the aborted fetus was quite simply "the point" of being itself, the winning point in the game, key point in the argument, a point tragically and stupidly conceded to the philosophical nothingness and cultural emptiness which encroach at every level. In Atwood's Hemingwayan quest the empty space of the protagonist's womb acquires grim personification as death itself until the lost child surfaces in vision as the protagonist's mother, god, grail, self. Mary Gordon's Felicitas, protagonist of *The Company of Women* (1980), suffers in vision this same presence: abortion is her death, death itself. She averts it, but only the many mothers of the company, recovered to her by her crisis, make the birth and survival of the new child and the new Felicitas possible.

Not until 1982, as the pro-life movement gathers momentum, do we find a full-throated cry for abortion rights in Marge Piercy's *Braided Lives*. This novel's stern and vulnerable poet-protagonist, undergoing at seventeen a nearly ruinous home abortion prepared by her fearful mother, lays the key on the table about the dark side of maternal desire: "Only I will know how I sometimes dream of that small changeling dribbling love on my breasts and how sick is that dream quivering with power. It would love me, poor bastard; it would have to."[1] The chapter in which this morally strict choice is made is called "The Agon."

All these novels are set in those prelegal days when abortion itself meant an intimacy with death for the woman as well as the fetus. The heroines mostly experience both the choice that ends in birth and the choice that ends in abortion as male plots, part of the network of "sick arrangements" (48), as Didion's protagonist calls them, by which patriarchy manipulates women, coming or going, into the structures of its normalcy.[2] The female counterplot inevitably turns on some kind of outlawry. Didion's Maria Wyeth and Atwood's nameless narrator skirt the edges of madness. Piercy's Jill Stuart forms an illegal abortion referral service. Even Gordon's Felicitas Taylor, who chooses against the abortion plot and makes a determined effort to adjust to "ordinary life. . . . the daughter of my mother, the mother of my daughter, caretaker of the property, soon to be a man's wife," wears that camouflage of the ordinary uneasily, afflicted still with a noble and "specific hunger" (267) for an as yet still alienated relationship with the absolute, with the sacred, with God.[3]

The female counterplot also strives to transform the deaths of ordinary life, aborted fetus, aborted woman, into life. "We are not dying" is the elated final judgment of Felicitas's once-endangered daughter on her once-endangered and still not fully-actualized mother. "Take my death inside. Give birth to me!" cries the specter of Jill's beloved cousin, Donna, dead in a self-induced abortion, and "I will," Jill answers. *Sine qua non*, the value of not dying, of giving birth, survives in these novels, whether attached to blood motherhood or not.

Play It as It Lays: Peril and the Point

In both Didion's 1970 novel and Atwood's 1972 novel the male characters make films of the female ones. In *Surfacing*, a novel of the primitive set in Canada, David and Joe are making a private film, taking "Random Samples" (their title) of the life and people they meet. Atwood makes this a pure symbol of male possessiveness, soul stealing as the old tribes would have called it. In *Play It as It Lays*, a novel of "sophisticated" Hollywood, the knowledgeable Joan Didion adds a further turn of the screw. The pure alienation associated with being made into film, into surface, the depthless emptiness revealed and confirmed by that process, may be "the answer," the truth about the human soul. Pregnancy/abortion is a reflection of this truth; pregnancy/birth is a miraculous, a romantically visionary, a poignantly crazy, refutation of it.

As *Play It as It Lays* begins, director Carter Lang has already made two films featuring his wife, the model turned actress, Maria Wyeth. In the first, a slice-of-life documentary like the one in *Surfacing*, the camera followed the then model around town: "Maria doing a fashion setting, Maria asleep on a couch at a party, Maria on the telephone arguing with the billing department at Bloomingdale's, Maria cleaning some marijuana with a kitchen strainer, Maria crying on the IRT. At the end she was thrown into negative and looked dead."[4] Carter's friend, the gay, nihilistic, male producer, BZ, has seen in this filmed figure, this rootless, disoriented, finally negatived woman, an existential kinship. By day BZ makes films and "does favors for people"; by night he plods expressionlessly the rounds of parties, obscurely grateful for the occasional episodes of temper, violence, vicious sex he sees. He watches the flesh-and-blood Maria, sucked helplessly into the same meaningless round, struggle away in terror from the complicit knowledge that all quests, all purpose, all L.A. freeways lead "to the quintessential intersection of nothing" (66). And he waits for her to join him and her filmed self in the negative surface of nonbeing: "You're getting there," BZ says as the novel's plot moves to its climax at a film site on the empty California desert. "Getting where?" "Where I am" (191).

BZ's nihilist quest ends with sleeping pills in a motel room on the desert, Maria's motel room. He comes to share his death with Maria "because you and I, we know something" and "because I wanted—." He leaves his last desire blank but lies down on the bed hand in hand with the female presence who thoroughly understands, will not argue, bids him sleep; and yet, as he begins to swallow the pills, out of some romantic, ridiculous, half-ashamed remembrance of her role as affirmer of life, murmurs, "Don't." The presence is mother.

Maria, in the same nihilist place as BZ, knows "what nothing means, and keep[s] on playing" (213), stays in the game. She is the mother of one living child, Kate, afflicted with Down's syndrome and institutionalized. From the "hospital" where she is being psychoanalyzed after being found on the bed with the dead producer, she announces in the first chapter, "What I play for here is Kate" (2). A second fetus, conceived with the ambiguously named Les Goodwin during a separation from her husband, confirmed Maria's existence in a place BZ could never be, "a realm of miseries peculiar to women" (61). Both Maria's journey to "the hard white empty core of the world" (161) and her quixotic, final rejection of the truth of nihilism—"Why? BZ would say. Why not, I say" (213)—turn on the grim and choiceless abortion of this fetus, which dominates the plot and ties together the metaphoric structure of the novel. The telephone, the plumbing, the road, the film, the game, above all "the point" converge in Maria's pregnancy/abortion.

Whether in a crap game or in philosophical argument you "make" your "point": meaning does not inhere, it is given, imposed. The doctors define Kate as damaged, unsalvageable. Questioning their meaning, Maria hears their unintelligible definition of the disease and its possible treatment—"Kate screamed. The nurse looked reproachfully at Maria. 'Methylphenidate hypochloride'."—and concedes, "All right. Your point" (71). BZ's wife subtly taunts Maria about Carter's affair with an actress, and Maria says, "You're missing the point." "Whose point?" Helene responds, and the reader gathers in all the points: Carter's and Helene's that they want to hurt Maria; Maria's that she can't care (138). Maria tries to revive her least destructive relationship with a man, the attraction to the aborted fetus's father, Les Goodwin. "Wrapped together like children" they contemplate staying together for another day, an hour, a minute, but the minute goes flat: "There's no point" (133). For Les, dimly goodhearted but committed to wife and career, there was never much point. For Maria, the rescuing point, not of that relationship but of relating at all, has been "left in a bedroom at Encino" (138) where the abortion arranged by men for the convenience of men took place.

Some of these arrangements go well, of course. Maria remembers a girl in New York whose friend in the DA's office had set one up as a quid pro quo: he arranged a legal D and C and she falsely testified to a grand jury that she had knowledge of a call girl operation, one woman betraying others, all of them manipulated by men (116). Once "this spirited perspective" (117) of quid pro quo had appealed to her. Now, "sick of everybody's sick arrangements" (48), she hears Carter, in his director's problem-solving mode, prepare "to give her the telephone number of the only man in Los Angeles County who did clean work," and hesitates.

> "Alright, don't do it. Go ahead and have this kid." He paused, confident in his hand. She waited for him to play it through. "And I'll take Kate." (54)

Maria's subsequent numbed sense that "everything was happening exactly the way it was supposed to happen" (54) parallels her continuing recognition that all her conversations with men are somehow replays of former conversations: the scenarios are written and fixed and she can maintain "only a distant interest in just how long the scene would play" (50). Carter genuinely thinks an abortion is necessary for Maria's mental health. His casual blackmail is as much the swift response of a confident director to a troublesome actress as it is the simple malice of a manipulating, soon-to-be ex-husband. Maria, wanting choice, already shaken by the entropic embrace of "nothing," cannot afford to risk her one hold on purpose, the child, Kate, and agrees to the arrangement.

Agreement triggers a dark night of the maternal soul from which she wakes "crying for her mother," the mother who had run her car off the road in a mysterious crash in the Nevada desert years before. The mother whose "yearnings suffused our life like nerve gas, *cross the ocean in a silver plane,* she would croon to herself, and mean it" (5). Recognition that she is going to destroy "the point" wakes memories of the never-quite-activated, the never-to-be-severed cord between herself and her own mother. News of her mother's death had precipitated a desirous fantasy: What was her mother

71

doing driving alone in Tonopah? Had she cracked up the car on purpose? Wouldn't her mother have tried to give her a last message?

> She imagined her mother trying to call her from a pay phone in Tonopah, standing in a booth with all her quarters and dimes and nickels spread on the shelf. . . . What time is it there, her mother would have asked had she gotten Maria. What's the weather. She might never have said what was on her mind but she would have left a coded message, said goodbye. (60)

Delivering details of "the arrangement" over the phone to Carter after suffering this fantasy again, Maria looks at herself in a mirror, "picking out her mother's features. Sometime in the night she had moved into a realm of miseries peculiar to women" (61), a realm of coded messages from mother to daughter-mother, which all say the same thing. "She can't win if she's not at the table, Francine," her father had said to her mother (86), approving eighteen-year-old Maria's ambition to go to New York to become a model. And again, after her mother dies: "Don't let them bluff you back there because you're holding all the aces" (7). The countermessage, spy coded in dreams over imaginary telephones, desert to desert, from despairing mother to despairing mother, is that the table is rigged, is *theirs:* "I mean, maybe I was holding all the aces, but what was the game?" (8).

Play It as It Lays depicts an entropic world splitting apart in the centripetal force of its own pointless speed and greed, held together by that alienating imitation of community and communication, the pay telephone. Rocketing from dismay to dismay, choiceless act to act, Maria often enacts the fantasy of "reach out and touch" she imagined from her mother as her death closed in. She stops at pay phones to initiate contact, ask for help, whisper "I love you" to the preoccupied ears of ex-lovers, dials a prayer just to "hear someone's voice" (64). Being near a phone seems at first like having a lifeline to rescue from the "unspeakable peril" of sheer existence, the death thread in the weave of things, from the "coral snake in the blanket" (1) that threatens especially mothers and children, that makes even mothers and children turn on each other. When the phone is out of order, or dread of peril drives one out of the house and onto the freeways, the pay phone is the last link with rescue: "The line at the pay phone in Ralph's Market suddenly suggested to Maria a disorganization so general that the norm was to have either a disconnected telephone or some clandestine business to conduct, some extramarital error. She had to have a telephone" (100). But the pay phone at the end of the freeway finally only connects her to the voice that asks flatly and familiarly, "How advanced is the *problem,* Maria?" (56) and offers the abortion as a solution to "the problem" of being: "Hear that scraping, Maria? . . . That should be the sound of music to you" (82).

Didion's novel offers perhaps the most extensive treatment of one of the most powerful images in abortion story making: It's never over when it's over; it's never gone, even when its product has been deposited in the toilet. The blood that could have been life, the tissue that could have been "the point," comes back. Maria hemorrhages for several weeks until her body ejects a portion of the placenta that the musical scraping did not reach, and memories of her own mother, "a little depressed" (85), "sick of you all" (88), continue their coded warning. Dreams begin in which "a shadowy Syndicate" traps her into a house all of whose plumbing backs up: "Of course, she could not call a plumber, because she had known all along what would be found in the pipes, what hacked pieces of human flesh" (96). When the sink in her house actually backs up, Maria moves out, but inevitably, months later, the shower in the rented room begins to drain too slowly. Sickened, stoically shouldering her burden, Maria moves back to her house: "There would be plumbing wherever she went" (103). There would also be dreams: "This way to the gas, ladies and gentlemen, a loudspeaker kept repeating. . . . And she would be checking off the names as the children filed past her. . . . Her instructions were to whisper a few comforting words to those children who cried or held back, because this was a humane operation" (125). The dreams didn't end until the day, six months later, when, unconsciously counting, she slumps over in her car, her refuge, in tears: "This was the day, the day the baby would have been born" (140).

The sentimental romance of this presentation, where the contents of Maria's womb is "a child in peril" from before its conception (because of its link with Maria's living but endangered child, Kate) to its damaged visionary birth and in dreams forever after, is countered, I think, by the extreme spareness of the novel's narrative, structure, and ethos. The child in peril is a fiction "conceived" gallantly to give "point," mass, direction, in the winds of emptiness that sweep the soul, to name that which stands against existential despair. In the humanist tradition child has always been the name of that value. The additional feminist accusation made here is that men, having no innate maternity to allow them, force them to harbor "the point," no visceral urgency to conceive meaning, future, in the teeth of the nihilist answer, are therefore helpless against (BZ), in witless league with (Carter), or actively lovers of the winds of emptiness. They betray woman the point maker, child as the point, to the peril.

Most of the novel's men are unconscious embracers of emptiness. Dimly smug, they profit from the peril. Their attitudes range from the futile good fellowship of Les Goodwin, to the game ignorance of Maria's father and her godfather, Benny Austen (who stay in the game simply because they are gamblers, not because, like the women, the point they make is human), to the sublime obtuseness of Maria's husband, Carter. In the one chapter the novel gives to a male voice, Carter seeks some order, a pattern "leading to the madness" by which his wife disarranged the well-meant arrangements of his marriage—her (his) abortion and the linked suicide of their friend, BZ—replaying scenes in his director's mind, trying to cut and compose meaning.

> Another scene: she is playing on the lawn with the baby, tossing up drops of water from a clear plastic hose. "Watch out she doesn't get chilled," I say from the terrace; Maria looks up, drops the hose, and walks away from the baby toward the poolhouse. She turns, and looks back at the baby. "Your father wants to talk to you," she says. Her voice is neutral. (12)

To his own uncomprehending ears Carter's warning is merely humane, as Mr. Ramsay's warning that "it won't be fine" for a trip to the lighthouse is merely common sense in Virginia Woolf's novel.

What the mother heard (and the child, too, if the analogy with the opening scene of *To the Lighthouse* holds) was the voice of the peril itself, threatening, manipulating, replacing the mother's water-bearing play with the father's chill-giving direction.

A few men are conscious instruments of the peril, recruiters for it. One is Larry Kulick, an active decadent, reportedly "a lawyer for gangsters" (25), who, like BZ, recognized Maria's entropic drift and sought to hasten it with invitations to his stereophonic orgies. Another is Ivan Costello, a former lover, a grimly inert decadent, a veritable black hole, whose seduction of Maria went like this:

> I want to tell you right now I'm never going to do anything again. There's not going to be any money and there's not going to be any eating breakfast together and there's not going to be any getting married and there's not going to be any baby makes three. And if you make any money, I'll spend it. (141)

The young Maria, foolishly courting the peril, agreed, but hesitated, speculating that if she did get pregnant and he left, "at least I'd have a baby." "No you wouldn't," he had said in a tone whose mystic import, thwarting male to point-making female, Maria only registers the day after her baby by Les Goodwin would have been born.

The novel's structure, a jump cut montage of three, short monologues and eighty-four, one-to-three-page scenelets and voice-overs, duplicates the suspect technology of the motion picture, rescuing it, in a turn of the screw, from its male controllers. The first and last voices are Maria's, a voice of authenticity speaking from the madhouse, a guilty murderess waking in her cell to concentrate on the child she rescued from the peril of its father by sacrificing the aborted child. Yet, final turn of the screw, there is an undertow even to these minimalist rescues of the film and the point. The rhetoric of filmmaking, "shoot," and especially "cut," permeates the text, from Carter and ultimately from Maria. In extremity, "a radical surgeon of my own life" (202), Maria becomes an editor of her own film: "Never discuss. Cut." Yet this role abuts a more dangerous analogue, bitterly recognized and accepted: "In that way I resemble the only man in Los Angeles County who does clean work" (202)—the abortionist.

From this point of view it is necessary to note the disappearance of Kate, the first child, the only protected point, from the narrative. When Maria begins to tell the reader her story, her voice and plan are confident: "I bother for Kate. What I play for here is Kate. Carter put Kate in there and I am going to get her out" (2).[5] By voice-over seventy-eight the tone has changed: "Nobody bothers me. The only problem is Kate. I want Kate." In poignant voice-over eighty-two the desire has the air of a dream: "My plans for the future are these: (1) get Kate, (2) live with Kate alone, (3) do some canning. Damson plums, apricot preserves. Sweet India relish and pickled peaches. Apple chutney" (209). By the finale, voice-over eighty-four, Kate is absent. Only the canning image remains in the narrator's image of her dream: "On the whole I talk to no one. I concentrate on the way light would strike filled Mason jars on a kitchen windowsill" (213). If the minimalist rescue of meaning is still in being here, it requires us to see Kate, the point, somehow as safely, invisibly enclosed, a plum in the filled Mason jar.[6]

Surfacing: "We Will Have to Begin"

A suggestive image, light striking a filled Mason jar. Filled with what? Plums, apricots, or perhaps, below the level of language, hidden from peril, a fetus? In Margaret Atwood's 1972 novel *Surfacing*, a woman brings to the level of consciousness and narrative, with great trauma, the abortion her married lover compelled her to undergo. It first takes the image of a fetus in a bottle, staring out of huge jelly eyes, until she can bear the truth that her fetus never had even the honor of a bottle, but was, like Maria's, "scraped . . . into a bucket" and thrown into the sewers (168).[7] This grim image is countered, however, by the medieval-mystic one, both early (34) and later (185, 223) in the novel, of the preborn child as a live, observing, human animal, protected like a frog in a jar, like a goldfish in a bowl, "able to look out through the walls of the mother's stomach" (38).[8]

What do these eyes see? When a child, the narrator drew that picture: the baby gazed out of the mother's "round moon stomach" at a man with "horns on his head like cow horns and a barbed tail" (185), Jesus in Mary's womb observing God as a threatening male.

Before the narrator dives to this mythic depth, however, the novel presents a world like the one Didion depicts, alienated from its deeps by the addiction of humanity to surfaces which can be shot, cut, and edited.

The unnamed, female narrator goes into the Canadian woods to find her suddenly missing father, accompanied by her lover, Joe, their friends, David and Anna, and hundreds of feet of film on which the men are capturing random samples of interesting objects: a house made of pop bottles, a gutted fish. This seems an apparently harmless fancy until the monomaniacal eye of the camera begins projecting the real desire of its "shooter" to seek human prey. On a spontaneous whim that reflects their true nature, Joe and David decide to make a dual "cameo appearance" carrying a log they chopped in the woods but find they can't both carry the log and "shoot." They won't give up the camera's eye to either of the women and end up separately "shooting" each other "standing beside the axe buried in the log, arms folded, and one foot on it as if it were a lion or a rhinoceros" (98).

The men are hunters; their art is predatory. The woman is an artist, an illustrator, but she is uneasy with art's innate aggression, self-reflexiveness, denial. Trained by a teacher-lover who gave her C's and D's to "build her character" (that is, reduce it), the narrator has brought with her a book of Canadian folk tales to illustrate for her publisher; but her attempts to capture reality, especially the ambiguous and finally damaging truth about the princesses in those cautionary tales, has set her to exploring the myth and not images of it, the wreck and not the story of the wreck. Finally she abandons drawing to be drawn into the truths of the tales.

The men keep those truths at bay, beneath surface, by investing in, manipulating, images. In a later sequence the two men turn on/to the narrator's friend, Anna, for "material": "We need a naked lady [for] Random Samples" (159). They force her to undress for the ultimate, alienated "capture" as surface. Under pressure, knowing from a long and damaging marriage that she keeps David's love only by spirited fights which rouse him followed by abject capitulations which satisfy him, Anna complies with both desires. The camera, which swiveled and trained on her "like a bazooka" (160), captures

Anna naked but giving David the finger, swearing but weeping. When the narrator, deep in a private world of myth, unwinds the film at the end of the novel and feeds it to the lake, all the captured images seem to "swim away like tadpoles" (195), released from alienated surface into the living depths; a climax to the feminist counterplot which evokes but reverses the earlier traumatic image of the narrator's aborted fetus dumped dead into the city's sewers.

Maria Wyeth's trauma emanated not only from the loss involved in the abortion but also from a sense of her own complicity in the "sick arrangements" which her world substitutes for the saving fictions of coherence, which the lost child symbolized. So, too, does Atwood's Canadian narrator nearly crack under her complicity with "the Americanization," the mechanization, of the planet. Only halfway through a brilliantly deceptive, first person narration does the reader recognize that the protagonist's life did not pivot on the feminist resistance to narrow, wife-mother roles which appears to mark her behavior now.

> What upset them was the way I did it, so suddenly and then running off and leaving my husband and child, my attractive full-color magazine illustrations, suitable for framing. . . . But I couldn't have brought the child here. I never did identify it as mine. It was my husband's; he imposed it on me. . . . He wanted a replica of himself. (34, 39)

That whole story was a slick "illustration" falsifying the shabby truth. There was no child; only an abortion imposed by a smug, married lover who wanted no "baby makes three," and accepted by a frightened, anxiously loving, finally self-degraded female.

In *Surfacing* the narrator's recovered memory of mechanized birth—"They don't let you see, they don't want you to understand. They want you to believe it's their power, not yours. . . . Your legs are up on a metal frame, they bend over you, technicians, mechanics, butchers" (96)—is itself a cover story for the still grimmer truth. Men desire love without fear, sex without risk, pregnancy without birth, pure mechanism, the Lawrentian nightmare. Rejecting the mystic potency of animal being, humanity, led by the male, the "American," is choosing a terrible metamorphosis.

> They're hulking out of the boat now, four or five of them. I can't see them clearly, their faces, the stems and leaves are in the way; but I can smell them, and the scent brings nausea, it's stale air, bus stations and nicotine smoke, mouths lined with soiled plush, acid taste of copper wiring or money. Their skins are red, green in squares, blue in lines, and it's a minute before I remember that these are fake skins, flags. Their real skins above the collars are white and plucked, with tufts of hair on top, piebald blend of fur and no fur like moldy sausages or the rumps of baboons. They are evolving, they are halfway to machines, the leftover flesh atrophied and diseased, porous, like an appendix.
> (215)

Deep in the forest, the narrator at the end of the novel watches her own kind come in helpful search for her. She sounds like Conrad's Marlowe in *Heart of Darkness*, briefly experimental, taking the point of view of the cannibals about his own kind, but Atwood's female Kurtz has dived deeper and tells no lies in the end. The horror is not in the jungle or in the revelation of the animal sources of being or even in the revelation of humanity's blasphemous drive to godhood. To her these things are good. The horror is the self-devouring impulse, the willed self-fragmentation, the machine desire: horrors embodied in the abortion.[9]

The narrative constructs the abortion at the matrix of a series of descents into the novel's watery heart of darkness. Seeking her missing father, the narrator comes back from America to the Canadian lakeshore home she left. She "remembers" that her brother drowned; she imagines that her father, tracking the primitive, animal rock paintings he had become interested in, dived too deep near the base of the cliff and drowned. She moves toward the water which contains the fish she and her friends need to eat to survive. But standing at the edge, looking at her feet "white as fish flesh on the sand" (86), she begins increasingly to identify with the beleaguered animal kingdom, hunted now not for food but for fun by

Americans intent on the mass destruction ("the ones who stuffed the pontoons of their seaplane with illegal fish, the ones who had a false bottom to their car, two hundred lake trout on dry ice" [14]) which is their expression of power.

Hating Americans, David pontificates on the nineteenth-century American exploitation of Canadian resources: "Do you realize . . . that this country is founded on the bodies of dead animals? Dead fish, dead seals, dead beavers . . ." (46). But beneath his radical politics he is himself an American, worshipping death, and the narrator, recoiling, separates herself from her kind at the end of part 1: "Finally being in the air is more painful than being in the water, and I bend and push myself reluctantly into the lake" (87).

The novel's first section, deceptively intimate in first person, present tense narrative, was lies: about her "husband," her "child," her brother, her father. The second section, cautiously exploratory in first person, past tense, begins with lies: "At my wedding we filled out forms. . . . I could recall the exact smells. . . . It was a hot day . . . there was a flock of draggled pigeons pecking at the scuffed post office lawn beside the fountain. The fountain had dolphins and a cherub with part of the face missing" (105). But the lies painfully give way to truth. "It wasn't a wedding," she admits, "there were no pigeons. . . . The cherub with half a face was from the company town, I'd put it in so there would be something of mine" (169).

Like Maria Wyeth this protagonist has denied her loss and her complicity, constructing a fiction. It was her lover, not her husband, who had said, "It's over. Feel better?" And not about the wedding, but about the abortion. This truth surfaces in a carefully wrought self-exorcism which begins when the narrator dives to look for her father's rock paintings, imagining he had left her coded instructions where to find them, and finds instead, "drifting toward me from the farthest level where there was no life, a dark oval trailing limbs" (169). It might be her father, drowned questing; she hoped it was her brother (but in fact she admits her mother had rescued him in that "remembered" incident). Then it becomes her aborted fetus, her potential self, her child self, the Lawrentian animal connected with the universal springs of mystery and power, the Canadian foundation of being which is still seeking "sanctuary" from "American" technicians of death. And in an important enlightenment, one that links her, as we shall see, with the protagonist of Toni Morrison's *Beloved*, the woman accuses herself: "I let them catch it . . . that made me one of them too, a killer" (170).

This "talisman" from her father—the primitive animal paintings, the awakening triggered by his dead body—offers the narrator a new vision. Rooted now in totemic animal power, she becomes fully aware of the self-destructive mechanism of "the humans" and fully alive to what they threaten and deny: the lines of "power" emanating from water, field, root, and creature. Seeking a further coded message from her father, "Not only how to see but how to act" (179), she follows these lines of power to a forgotten drawing of her own childhood, in which a child inside a woman stares out at a horned man-god, the aggressor. She had read and acted out the terror of that vision all her life; now she acts out the power of it. As the novel's second section ends, the first person, present tense active voice returns, and she eyes her lover, Joe, no longer the horned and hostile man-god but an as yet unactualized human "for whom truth might be possible" (186), for whom "perhaps I am the entrance, as the lake was the entrance for me" (172).

As the third section begins, the narrator draws Joe out to the woods for sex, the archetypal entranceway for god, meaning, and feels "my lost child surfacing within me, forgiving me, rising from the lake" (191). The imagined child inside becomes a god, and she, in a forty-page section at the novel's visionary heart of darkness and light, suffers a spell of lucid madness, reducing herself to animality, roaming the forest naked, fasting and purified, enthralled. She is reconnected to her dead mother and father: both figures appear in this vision gazing beyond her or each other towards some mysterious reality in the distance. Rerooted in motherhood and daughterhood, the narrator becomes at last the harbor of fluid divinity in a world drained, self-drained, of meaning. A savage madonna, she plots an incarnation (not for nothing is her lover named Joe) and receives the annunciation in a pagan pastorale: "wolf's eyes, depthless but lambent. Reflectors. . . . A fish jumps, carved wooden fish with dots painted on the sides, no, antlered fish thing drawn in red on cliffstone. . . . flesh turned to icon, he has changed again. . . . How many shapes can he take?" (218–19).

This, for a woman who followed her father from early childhood in rebellion against the blue ceramic madonnas and twisted roadside crucifixions of the surrounding French Catholic tradition, would seem a kind of defeat, did the novel not have a final move left. After the magically filled image, the emptied one: "It becomes an ordinary fish again" (219). You track the wolf-god into the heart of darkness and, returning exultant from the granted vision, find it originated where all visions of power originate: "No gods to help me now, they're all questionable once more, theoretical as Jesus. They've receded, back to the past, inside the skull, it is the same place" (221).

Yet the domain of the sacred, degraded, parodied, totemized, banalized, remains, as we say now, "sous erasure," the ground of the narrator's discovery and self-recovery. "No total salvation, resurrection" (221) do the gods, receding, give. But the lost child, surfacing mythically, forgives: redemption, self-transforming, occurs. "To become like a little child again, a barbarian, a vandal" is the wrong path, the narrator muses, the one "the Americans" of all nationalities and both genders have taken. No, "redemption was elsewhere" (156). Redemption is to become (like) a mother, child gazing out from the belly, gods gazing out from the skull.

Whether the sex performed half in madness but at the right time of the month has conceived a real child or not, whether the god locus of power now back in the skull was "seen" or not, "I assume it," says the narrator, choosing the word carefully for its two meanings, take for granted and take on. So armed, or rather, inhabited, by the personal power she now must admit she has and must use, she re-enters her own time at the end of the novel, taking up the bewildered and resentful lover, Joe, "half-formed," like another fetus. When she was a child, she says, the French Catholic children "terrified me by telling me there was a dead man in the sky watching everything I did and I retaliated by explaining where babies come from" (52). The novel depicts not the rejection of the first explanation of power from the skies for the second, of power from the body, but rather the internalizing and fusing of the two. Having "recanted . . . the old belief that I am powerless" in the gaze of the dead man in the sky or the living men wishing mechanical sex without risk, the woman steps forward, source of her own power, the inner eyes of the child-god focused on the waiting lover, the present time, the ordinary world: "We will have to begin" (224).

The Company of Women: Child as Change

Emphatically children of their time, the 1960s, the protagonists of *Play It as It Lays, Surfacing,* and *The Company of Women* respond to its key message: "They all disowned their parents . . . the way you are supposed to," as *Surfacing*'s narrator expresses it. Yet in the crisis of identity, the near madness consequent on the complicity with male-enforced abortions, the women of the earlier novels refind their children and themselves in visionary response to the coded messages of their dead mother's lives. Maria Wyeth's mother cracked up her car in the desert battling the nameless peril, but she sang her message round the house: "Fly the ocean in a silver plane, See the jungle when it's wet with rain." *Surfacing*'s narrator recalls her mother wanted to fly, too, though as a child the mother broke both ankles trying to fly from the barn rooftop (146). Maria's mother was isolated in a male world, and so is she; Atwood's heroine has only one suborned and desperate female friend and her mother only one sympathetic sister in a world of uncomprehending "madames." But Charlotte Taylor, the mother of Mary Gordon's protagonist, Felicitas, dwells in a fluidly life-enriching network, a "company" of women whose fused maternal instinct crosses the boundary of lives and generations. Pregnant, silent, in conscious rejection of her mother, her femininity, and that dangerously female and Catholic "company," the intellectualized and politicized Felicitas comes home to what she expects will be the accusations and rejections of her mother and finds herself enrolled, willy-nilly, in "the company."

> "We'll have to go away someplace and have it," she said.
> This was the beginning of her entirely appropriate use of
> the first person plural in relation to my pregnancy. (248)

Felicitas's fatalistic acceptance of this first person plural completes the pivotal scene of Gordon's 1980 novel in which the protagonist, watching women come and go in the abortionist's office, sees, in a vision as primitive and mythic as anything in *Surfacing*, another first person plural, another company of women, and rejects it.

> Someone had made a footprint in the blood that had come from the woman's body. The print had repeated itself to the door. Felicitas stared, trying to discover if it was the woman stepping in her own blood, or the driver, pulling her so that she could not be incriminating evidence. . . . And then Felicitas saw it: all the dead women, hacked and bled, eyes closed in a violent death because they preferred to die rather than to give birth. . . . And she could see herself there, dying in the back of a movie theater, in the ladies' room in the subway. She could feel herself losing her life. . . . She looked at the poor sad doctor. "I'm sorry," she said. "I've changed my mind." (235–36)

Strikingly, the vision of hacked flesh that makes abortion a moral abomination is not fetus's flesh, as in the first two novels, but women's flesh (as it will be, with quite different emphasis, in the Marge Piercy novel). In Gordon's novel pregnancy signals the fated fall of woman from the singularity which Felicitas first struggled to construct for herself, into the first person plural.[10] Birth will confirm that woeful if ambiguous life-giving plurality, but abortion will not, in this view, restore the precious singularity. Rather it would link her in another fellowship—with death. Either company means loss. For Felicitas, the vision of abortion—"she could feel herself losing her life" (236)—exactly matches the first reality of the birth of her child: "I understood mothers who want to take their babies' lives. It is life they must punish, for cheating them, for trapping them in the oldest trick in the world, the female body, for telling them, often children themselves, 'you are tied to this life now; your life is over'" (246).

And the only question left unanswered is, *who* is responsible for the no win situation? Whose footprint repeats itself in the blood of women? The man who would remove the "incriminating evidence" of pregnancy, sexuality? Or the woman who would wade through blood rather than accept the diminished singularity, the fated plurality which Life, with a capital *L*, imposes on mothers?

Analyzing "plurality," "company," as a fall, Mary Gordon nevertheless writes out of a tradition which likes to recoup the notion of
fall with the theology of the felix culpa—the happy fall, happy in
that the changes it imposes are the source of grace. In Gordon's
world, as in Atwood's, the compelling and contradictory signposts
of Catholic culture lie all around the protagonist, offering with one
hand what they take away with the other, organizing reality in ways
hard not to duplicate or parody even in the act of escape or denial
and containing redemptive potential even when they appear most
degraded. The allegory of the fall of Felicitas, Happiness, from the
singularity celebrated and enforced by the multiple mothers who
are the novel's first company, contains its rising action, too, signified
above all by the narrative's paradoxical structure. The first part
stresses, in expertly crafted, free, indirect discourse, the interwoven
lives of five women in the 1930s and 1940s; part 2 is intensely
focused on a single year, 1969–70, in the densely described, omnis-
ciently narrated experience of a single woman, Felicitas; part 3
brilliantly evokes, in intimate present tense, first person monologues, the individual realities of seven persons living in company
in 1977.

The novel's title word, "company," is full of ambiguities about the
singular and the plural. In canon law a priest forswears "the company of women"—erotic and familial life—to enter "a company of
strangers" (46)—male, gathered in silence and individual inner solitude around a central, male, triune God. The novel's Father Cyprian recoiled from all flesh, especially his own, in devotion to a God
imagined as "clear transparency" (47): refined even out of singularity, his God does not even stop light. The young, Catholic
working women who gathered around him in the 1930s—Clare,
Mary Rose, Muriel, Elizabeth, and Felicitas's mother, Charlotte—
responded to this vision of a hypersolitary God and to Cyprian personally because of a deeply, culturally infused worship of "that
something in men one could not touch, despite the attempts wom-
en made with their clean, warm houses, their protecting furniture,
their beds and open bodies" (10). "The hard, durable pride of such
company" (10), the company of the men who express that godlike
solitariness, knits the women together as much as does the consid-

erable mutual curiosity, support, the intuitive "we" that their natures express as a desire for the company of other women. Charlotte, Elizabeth, and Mary Rose feel this bond most of all; Clare, taking to heart Cyprian's precious compliment about her "mind like a man's" (23), feels it less; and Muriel, manlike in bitter withholding and bitter jealousy, feels it least of all.

Only by a very powerful act of denial does Cyprian, the priest, hold himself apart in singularity from the encroaching "we," the "company" (whether of men, of women, or of women and men) that humanizes, that measures one's distance from godhead. Over the years church reform strengthens the "we" not only between priests but between priests and ordinary people, threatening the security of his denial: "Togetherness is not found in canon law," he rages (49). He leaves his preaching order for a nomadic and partly degraded life as a secular priest, preaching part-time. His company of women, "perfectly faithful" (48), bear with him and with each other, subconsciously reforming themselves, with him, around another center of solitude and singularity, Felicitas, the only living child of any of them, of all of them.

At first, as a child, Felicitas lived in emotional alliance with the priest, acting out the "seriousness" about life that his enraged and intellectually critical apartness represents and delighting in the singularity which his love, his company, even his criticism, affords her. As an adolescent, Felicitas slowly begins to feel the pull of the "we," to feel the unnaturalness, the fictiveness, of the way she has been set up as the special, the nearly messianic, hope of the company. Above all she begins to understand the pernicious gender division which will forever keep her "the other" (42) to Cyprian, always looking at "the golden backs" (40) of priests and never on the altar, no matter how much his child, his alter ego, she aspires to be. At age twelve, briefly in the hospital with a flirtatious teenager, self-named "Gidget," who has bought into and expresses the "we" of adolescent adulthood, Felicitas suffers her first alienation from her singularity and his. She betrays him and herself, she feels, by joking about him in an effort to join Gidget in "the company" of teenagers.

This poignantly absurd betrayal, reconciled in a kind of baptism scene near a well which ends part 1, sets up the massive alienation in part 2 when the seventeen-year-old Felicitas, attracted to the counterculture of 1969–70 during her freshman year at Columbia University, rises in rebellion against her "father" and her mothers, defines and excoriates the diminishment of their plurality—and then duplicates it. Cyprian's honorable, man-defining singularity she now sees as needy, ragged loneliness: "Without their shelter he would wither." The older women's intellectual choice of a spiritual mentor she now sees as a mere "act of female instinct." She thinks "the lives of the women she knew were bankrupt. . . . The women had forgotten themselves, forgotten what they stood for. Now they stood for Cyprian, they stood around him, because he was a man, and wounded. . . . why did they need it so, a man to lie to? . . . So that he would not have to see the truth [that] without their shelter, he would wither" (98).

Seething with contempt for the female compromises of her mother's generation, Felicitas constructs a new "free" life as an antitype of the old one. Its foundation, too, is a lie to a man; its structure a company of women. She falls hard for her political science teacher, Robert Cavendish, a man in trendy revolt against his privileged Anglo-Saxon background and its bourgeois "hang-ups" over possessions and possessiveness. She sleeps with him, recentering her life, as he directs, as "the sixties" direct, on erotic freedom: "Now she was doing something that would bring her to the center of the world" (129). Moving in with Robert, she becomes one of a commune trio of women who live the fiction of total, possessionless, sexual freedom, each woman hiding her monogamous desire for the undivided honor of the man's sexual company.

Gordon designs several scenes in this section to show how similar the spiritual and the sexual communes are: women in each case speechless before the chosen and choosing man, but growing closer to one another; the man in each case slowly revealing his emptiness. As Cyprian desired to lose his male flesh in the solitary transparency of the spirit, so Robert speaks of his wish to lose his wealth and even his gender. To experience life in the fullest way, he says, he would like to be a suffering black woman, to sing like Billie Holliday (115).[11] Yet both men rely with sublime duplicity on the culturally grounded privilege of the manhood they pretend to renounce. Cyprian, joking with a Christmas present, puts a tiny gun to Felicitas's head and asks her to kneel while he pulls the trigger. It turns out to be a cigarette lighter, but it was not wholly a joke, and Felicitas, hating her instinctive obedience and him, knows it. Robert, asking her to demonstrate fidelity to the free-sex canon of the commune, orders her to have sex with a male friend, Richard, and Felicitas, hating her obedience and the lie of nonmonogamous desire—"You want me to want it, but you don't want me to want *you*" (198)—begins to disintegrate psychically. To be Cyprian's hope as a child, to be Robert's lover and therefore Cyprian's anti-hope as a young woman, was to retain individual personality; to be both Robert's *and* Richard's lover is to lose it.

The pregnancy that ensues demonstrates that the price of total obedience, boundarylessness, immersion in "we" with no hard atom of an "I," is surrender to a frantic series of timeless and impersonal roles: "How odd," she thinks, listening to the doctor's jargon as he confirms his diagnosis, "I'm a person who has regular sexual contacts" (216); "She was no longer herself, she was a pregnant woman" (218); "Now she was one of those girls [who] gave birth in secret, where the babies were taken from them or kept from them" (220). As the choice approaches, "She could no longer imagine herself as anyone interested in the embraces of some man. It had been an odd disease, her adoption of sexual interest, but it was over now. She would never be that person again. Now she was a person who had to have an abortion. After that she did not know who she would be" (221–22). Pregnancy, in an old dark typology, becomes, like Cyprian's lighter, the gun at her head. On the day she chooses against what she sees as death by abortion, the day the United States invades Cambodia, she envisions the singular and independent person she used to be, wanted to be, joining the spontaneous demonstration against the war that goes down one street. She goes down another, towards her mother, towards the hated female company, for "there was no place for her" among the demonstrators. "She was going to have a child" (237).

Felicitas's conviction that the life of the person she *was* has ended with pregnancy is true. That person, a kind of holy child carrying every magic potentiality of intellect, spirit, and achievement which her mothers and "father" imagined, disappears, inevitably, when one of those potentialities—and that one, unexpectedly, the oldest, most ordinary one—is actualized. This is Gordon's point, admitted to by the woman Felicitas becomes in the next seven years, as she slowly wakes into, then avidly seeks to confirm, the "ordinary" life which her name, "the one virgin martyr whose name contained some hope for ordinary human happiness" (3), promised on the surface and withheld at the core. Cyprian imagined her in the company of virgins dedicated to intellectual and spiritual achievement; Robert's imagined company, antivirgins wedded to an intellectual principle of erotic freedom, is a parody of this. The company in the abortionist's office, "sitting in orange chairs in various stages of distress" (230), and in all abortion situations back through time, are in Felicitas's vision virgin martyrs, too, since they preferred to die rather than give birth. Though the women Gordon puts in the New York abortionist's office in 1970 have, every one, a history of abuses or pregnancies or poverty that makes abortion a sympathetic choice for them, abortion becomes in this novel a symbol of the refusal to surrender potentiality to actuality, a denial of the necessities of change. "Troubled by human change," its unpredictable gift of "loss or healing" (255), Felicitas denied her change, her motherhood, through the birth and the first year of her daughter's life, "sheltering" the last vestige of the virgin self, the "I," against the remorseless and terrifying plurality of mother and child.

And it is terrifying. This extension of the self makes it deeply vulnerable to the peril that Maria Wyeth and the narrator of *Surfacing* felt all about them, a peril which is here, as everywhere, associated with men. "Is it unusual, my sense of danger?" the twenty-six-year-old Felicitas muses. "Surely all women are born knowing the men they love could kill them in a minute, that we are kept alive by kindness, that we are always in peril. This is the source of our desire for obedience, for the inherited knack, the alert readiness—even in women who rage or live their lives in solitude—for giving in" (245). In this sense, the novelist suggests (dangerously, perhaps), the woman who will not give in to change, to choice, to actuality, and finally, warily, to men is part of the peril—to herself and other women and children.

Felicitas describes how, dimly understanding, the company of her "mothers" gathered round her as a pregnant woman, as a young withholding mother, literally teaching her, like a human scientist a defective mother gorilla, the gestures and feelings of love, of motherhood and of self-mothering, until those gestures and feelings awoke in her. Finally welcoming "the gravitational pull of the baby I hadn't wanted to touch" (256), Felicitas understands that this force embeds her permanently in change. A third generation child gives the first "company," now grandmothers, "leave" to grow old and die (257). The birth of her daughter changes, or reawakens, the pattern of Felicitas's relationship with men. Since "a fatherless girl thinks all things possible and nothing safe" (263), Felicitas decides to marry the silent and protective Leo for Linda's sake and for her own, noting wryly the vestigial working of the desire for the "honor" of the company of man: "I wonder what abuse a woman has to go through at the hands of a man before she gives up the inward flicker of delight, like the click and flare of a cheap cigarette lighter, at being chosen? Where did we learn that definition of honor? As long as it is there, we are never really independent" (261).

The obverse of that flicker of delight is the swoon of fear/obedience when the cigarette lighter turns out to be the gun at the temple. There is no cure for this curse of the ordinary, this dark side of the plurality of women, except—but this is important—"a radical life" (260). The young Felicitas had caught glimpses of such a life. As a virgin and martyr, "I was singular," she recalls. Now motherhood and its pluralizing, boundary-obscuring roles may "make me lose my edge, will cover my bones in obscuring flesh, will move me from my desert landscape" (262). The images associated with the radical life—the singular, the bone, the desert—are starkly prepersonal, prenatal.

Although the novel depicts the inevitable birth of the bone of the "I" into the flesh of the "we," the "delivery" of the fictive singular into the real plural, the "fall" of the potential into the actual, some room is in fact left for the desert, the edge, the virgin. Felicitas's quest for the good and the beautiful, the lovingly human, is satisfied in her daughter, Linda. (The name, Spanish for "beauty," is philosophically significant, although she chooses it because, as the statistically most popular girl's name that year, it represents the safety of numbers, of the ordinary, for her child.) But she still yearns with "a specific hunger" for the sacred conceived as truth, not bliss; "light, not love" (267).

In Atwood's book sex and birth are hierogamous entrances, holy surfacings; abortion, male inspired, is denial of the sacred. In Gordon's book the call to birth is a simpler call to humanity, the ordinariness which may obscure, though it cannot eliminate, an opposite call. This opposite call, whose images are solid, not fluid, all edge, yields no drama of entrances, in this novel. Yet it does seem real, even though the male, the potentially perilous violator, is still at the center of this last visionary company:

> If I could see the face of God as free from all necessity, the vision as the reward of a grueling search, the soul stripped down, rock hard, then I would look for Him. If He would show Himself so, then I would seek Him. But I will not let Him into my heart. . . . I will not open my heart to God. If He is the only God I could worship, He will value my chastity." (267)

Braided Lives: Women Giving Birth to Women

Mary Gordon, though she can see the possibility of "a radical life," does not depict one. Marge Piercy does. *Braided Lives* is a flat-out feminist analysis of the fight for women's freedom and a call, in the face of the conservative rollback of the 1980s, for confirmation of the first article in that feminist bill of rights, reproductive freedom. The objects of the several abortions which braid the novel's plot are never understood to be babies, as in the other three books studied here. Pregnancy always symbolizes possession by one of the three forces—male lovers, the myth of motherhood, the truths of the female body itself—which in this society seek dominance over, instead of harmony with, the fourth force in life, the drive for female selfhood. The book is unashamed of its existence as argument but succeeds as a human story because of the passion of its argument, and because the protagonist sustains in the end a love for all humans: man and child as well as woman, for mother as well as self, for the body as integral with, and to, the will.[12]

But Jill Stuart bears no children. Her fertility and creativity takes the form of seven books of poems (Piercy herself had written seven volumes at the time of *Braided Lives*), and her human empathy takes the form of an increasingly confident participation in the right-to-life issues of the 1950s and 1960s: save the Rosenbergs, ban the bomb, feed the black children of Mississippi. And give life to women dying from botched abortions. Placed tellingly at the climax of the description of the self-induced abortion Jill barely survived at age seventeen in 1954 is this flash-forward to a birth differently chosen, fiercely wanted:

> Brooklyn, 1963. The doctor botched the abortion. She is hemorrhaging. I am one of a group of women who help other women secure abortions. . . . Now this woman, fat, gentle, in her late 30's and the mother of 5, is bleeding like a slaughtered pig—like I did. I pack her vagina with ice. I hold her against me, a woman twice my size and twice my body weight, and rock her like a baby. . . . Live, live, I whisper to her, dear one, sweetheart, angel darling, live. Only live. (223)

In her forties, a successful poet and lecturer, in the 1980s a feminist activist, Jill Stuart looks back on a life "braided," and abraded, with the lives of two key women, her mother and her cousin, Donna Stuart. "Were I pointing out a different pattern in the weave," the poet says, other women's lives would stand out as strands in the braid (416). But in this pattern the unifying topos is abortion; the central figures are the mother, who "is scared of the world and thinks if she punishes me first, I will be broken down enough to squeak through" (12), and the pretty blond cousin, "like negative and photo—me dark and you light" (234), who, like Jill's mother a generation before, tries to have her freedom within the complicit terms of, under the cover of, conformity to feminine stereotypes.

In the eight years of the novel's main focus—Jill's adolescence in Detroit, college in Ann Arbor, and early adulthood in New York

City—classic battles between mother and daughter break all but one thread of that strand. Her own birth, Jill speculates, both cause and result of that "love, cannibal love" (17), which is the other side of maternal self-denial, initiated the war. But the narrative of the forty-three-year-old Jill is rich with slowly surfacing insight about the unbreakable last thread, the desire between women, especially between mother and daughter, for a final non-cannibal form of love. The daughter's understanding of the mother increases: "She is a figure shaped by troubles I will never have to know. Sometimes I do listen, even if what I hear isn't what she is trying to tell me" (166). As time goes on, understanding offers both a warning and a healing.

> A year goes by while she never takes a cigarette out. Then one evening after supper on a day that feels no more un-usual than any other, she appears with a slender brown cylinder cupped elegantly between her fingers, acting in her own movie. Then I see in her the young beauty from the slums, studying seductive graces in darkened theaters. All she had to save herself was encompassed in being female. (177)

Having thus internalized "femininity" from the movies, from American culture of the thirties and forties, Jill's mother sensed the danger as her daughter grew up rough, self-motivated, ambitious for education, mysteriously committed to the uncertain life of a writer, and desirous of the rich and sometimes dangerous experiences that feed a writer's omnivorous imagination. The battle to "break" her daughter to the accepted female stereotype emerges from fear for her. What it bred in Jill was a ferocious desire to make her own choices: "I will escape you all. I will choose what I do" (225). Mother and motherhood, even daughterhood, become the enemy of choice-defined self. Rejecting all such ready-made roles, Jill nevertheless wins the beauty with the cigarette—the fear-ridden, punishing mother, the woman born into troubles—with the rock-bottom identity of poet and lover she creates for herself.

> My mother; the miracle is that in middle age we are friends. . . . Why did she stop disapproving of me? She

likes the row of books. . . . Now that I am in my forties, she tells me I'm beautiful . . . and we have the long, personal, and even remarkably honest phone calls I always wanted so intensely I forbade myself to imagine them. . . . I am deeply grateful. With my poems, I finally won even my mother. The longest wooing of my life. (527–28)

This relationship ends in lifegiving friendship, though its adult phase began with the devouring mother, witchlike and deadly, fearing the silent, destroying force of the father but complicit with his values, enforcing on the pregnant, seventeen-year-old daughter a home made abortion which nearly killed her.

The other key relationship in the braid ends in tragedy, though it began with physical and emotional love making between the thirteen-year-old cousins, Donna and Jill. Meeting again at college, the two women form a nonsexual, a metaphysical bond: "We strike against each other, chipping off the useless debris of our childhood. What one of us bites into, the other chews and swallows. . . . We define each other" (48). Donna, the blond, "negative" female image, anxious to move into the schizophrenic world of 1950s femininity, rushes into secret sex and forces herself into "love" and towards marriage with Jim, with Lennie, finally with Peter. Jill, Piercy's "positive" female image, reluctantly follows, imitating, with Mike, with Peter, with Kemp, finally with Howie. Donna fits her body into "iron-maiden bras" (251) and high-heeled shoes, brightly and consciously seeking freedom through "accepting my destiny as a woman" (431), while inexplicable rages of resentment and self-loathing overpower her regularly: one of them results in her death by self-induced abortion. Jill, seeking to center life "on some good work you want to do" (431), experiences obsessions, loneliness, failures, but survives as the "scavenger," the "alley cat," finally the artist that she wants to be.

In this leapfrogging, braiding, finally diverging relationship between women, abortion is the key symbol for both Donna's and Jill's kind of "freedom." First to enter a sexual relationship, Donna is first to fear pregnancy and seek money for an abortion. Trying to borrow money from her lover for this project, Jill finds him truculently "sid-

ing with the fathers . . . who say no to women" (162) on the basis
of sweeping generalizations about the sacredness of life. She responds, "That's just words. A fancy position for a man to take. I
mean it. I care about Donna. I'm willing for chickens and cows to die
to feed her, and this embryo to keep her free" (160).

Donna's plight turns out to be a false alarm this time, but later that
summer Jill takes Donna's place in the female predicament for real,
because she gave in to her lover's desire (he cited, poet to poet, man
to woman, the dictums about "the natural" from D. H. Lawrence) to
stop using condoms, "that damn armor" (168). Remembering his
earlier attitude, knowing he won't marry her and won't free her for
an abortion, Jill hides the fact from her lover, but her mother uncovers the truth. Obliquely hating/protecting her daughter, siding
with the father—"If you go roaming around to doctors, and you
can't trust a one of them, only in it for the money, I'll tell your father
and he'll make you have it" (210)—Jill's mother puts her through
several harrowing home remedies. Finally, while gunshots from the
father's TV western echo from the living room (the representation of
pregnancy as gun appears again) and her mother holds her mouth
to keep her silent, Jill carries out her choice in its enforced primitive
mode: "Now I will go to work attacking my body in earnest . . . by
force I open my womb" (218).

The rhetoric of attack Piercy uses here is carefully limited. It is not
herself or her life, or a fetal life identified with hers, or even with her
lover's that Jill feels she needs to attack. Rather it is the unruly body,
cells subdividing without her volition, which she needs to confront,
cherish, and rule, so that it can bear her free self. Jill had considered
suicide, but a powerful will to live and to experience the variety of
life dissolved that desire. After the abortion she lives a sexless life for
a time—"sex . . . seems to me a device for converting will and energy into passivity and flesh" (227)—but that kind of self-mutilation does not last either.

She makes friends with her body again through two simple expe-
dients: she buys a diaphragm—"my first passport, something
magical that permits passage out" (229)—and she begins to collect
the names of, and the personal funds for, competent abortionists for
herself and any other woman in danger. The following year, ready

to contract her upper-class dream marriage, Donna becomes pregnant after a rape from a lower-class hoodlum she had dated in one of her self-condemning fits of rage at herself and at that very dream. And Jill, deploring the feminine dream but steadfastly preserving Donna's freedom to pursue it, takes all necessary steps, even thievery, to procure money for an illegal but medically safe abortion.

It is interesting to note the ambiguous and important role of "the doctor" in this novel. He is cleanliness and training; he is safety, sought more heatedly than the lover, he is a necessary third presence in the procedure. Self- induced abortion, as represented here, seems much too close to suicide, not only pragmatically (the woman is untrained) but symbolically (the woman is deeply at odds with her own body). Yet he is still a man, not, finally, to be trusted.

This ambiguity locates itself in a metaphorical displacement, at a few key moments, of "the doctor" by "the dentist." At virtually the same time that she is helping Donna with the abortionist, Jill provides the money and the energy to get her mother to the dentist for work on her bad teeth. To the family's shock and rage, the dentist simply extracts all Mrs. Stuart's teeth, sound ones and decaying ones alike. The dire image of "dark blood welling" in the mouth here (373) recapitulates and anticipates the abortion motif. Both procedures, necessary to health yet associated with damage, performed by men for money on the bodies of women who submit not exactly from choice but to keep open the possibility of choice, combine elements of woe and success for the women who rage at them while desiring them. Jill helps a friend rob a dental supply store for Donna's abortion money. Later, fetus successfully aborted, engagement back on track, Donna persuades the wealthy, intelligent, handsome, and faintly sinister Peter Crecy to marry her quickly: "Fast is painless. Like pulling a tooth" (430).

Marriage for Donna is growing up, accepting womanhood, giving order to life. Her "work," she thinks, is her husband, Peter, a man in rebellion against his father and yet in training to be a junior patriarch just like him. Helpless to prevent it, sliding in her cousin/alter ego's wake towards marriage with Howie, her friend and lover, Jill watches Donna plan the compromises, engage in the psychic denials, of modern "femininity." She defines health as love and domesticity and the career in television news she clearly desires and thrives on as merely a temporary expedient until "the relationship" and its finances settle down. Peter has agreed, she thinks, to postpone children indefinitely, so when she finds a tiny hole in her diaphragm she responsibly buys a new one, celebrating at the same time the "instant respectability" that Jill attains when she announces her engagement to Howie.

Donna believes, genuinely, that Howie will "save" Jill, as Peter "saved" her, through marriage, from the "bad patterns," the disorderly-looking life— "Destroying myself. Ending up alone and crazy. Winding up a two-bit whore" (518)—which is the only alternative society can envision for unmarried women. The major breakthrough in Jill's artistic life, a new, personal, poetic voice freed by an encounter with the poetry of Alan Ginsberg, goes by unrecognized by anyone but herself as she leaves Donna, her "negative" twin, the bright but self-denied woman she wanted to truly save, in New York while she goes to Detroit to be inspected by prospective in-laws.

When Jill returns the novel's tragic climax has occurred. The death by abortion that has lain in the braided lives of women since the novel's opening, fended off at seventeen by Jill, is taken instead by the conflicted, compromised, self-loathing, twenty-three-year-old Donna, "grown up" to her schizophrenic and finally deadly destiny as a woman. The novel's last "rose of blood" blooms under Donna's body on the sheets of Jill's apartment. And Jill, notifying Peter of a death whose nature he somehow knows before he is told, remembering the "small hole, like a pinprick" (530) in Donna's diaphragm, grows "cold, cold through" (530), like the corpse on the bed. She believes he has pricked a hole in the diaphragm, deliberately made Donna pregnant without her consent or knowledge, killed her.

At the funeral it is all Jill can do to resist signing her name "Donna" in the visitors' book, so sunk is she in guilty identification with the lost twin, with the deadly archetype of femininity which Donna represents: the ancient fatality of women who either make a dead life bearing children to a betraying man, or who would rather die than give birth.

Separation from this archetype of femininity has been the struggle of Jill's life. A period of dreams and madness not unlike that undergone by the protagonist of Atwood's *Surfacing* climaxes at the novel's end with the mythic birth of a new and redeeming Donna. While Jill walks the night streets a bloody and ghostly Donna, "sharp ivory doppelganger," wails for entrance like some frail indestructible Catherine Earnshaw.

> "Leave me alone! Take me with you! It's cold and it hurts. It's getting colder. Mother. Make it stop! Momma! Momma!" "I will take you with me. I will!" "Take my death inside. Give birth to me!" "I will." (541)

Donna's voice, ambiguously that of child to mother, of aborting woman, or more deeply, of aborted woman, to self-saved woman, uses the ancient language of birth. Jill's "I will," unlike Heathcliff's, which signals his final obliterating immersion in his demon, represents not possession but parturition, the erasure of abortion as death, the inauguration of a wider motherhood. It crystallizes at the end the early image of woman giving birth to woman that rode under the enactment of Jill's abortion at seventeen. Its material embodiment is an underground network of safe abortion referrals called "Donna." This network functioned through the 1960s as that "small female government [of] conspirators and mutual advisors" (401) that Jill and Donna lived out in college together before Donna's choices, programmed by male lovers and her own entrapment in the myths of femininity, estranged them somewhat. Its spiritual legacy is a simple pledge in the teeth of mortality "to express my caring all the time" (546) to women and to men, and ultimately to the readers of her poems. Its practical result for Jill is a diffused and fractious loving which precludes traditional marriage and children of the blood, to spend itself on all the worthy human encounters of her life (at novel's end Jill is living, working, amiably quarreling with a long-term lover named Josh, and mothering Howie's daughter by another woman, as well as producing books and lectures).

As for the abortion freedom which paradoxically grounds this elliptical motherhood, this "death inside me" which makes births possible, both the narrator and the narrative structure argue force-fully for it. The bloody abortion that kills the protagonist's doppel-ganger at the climax does not contradict this. As a procedure which failed because its illegality made help impossible during the com-plications of aftermath, it stands starkly at one of the no exit gates—the other is death by immersion in unchosen maternity—of pa-triarchally-constructed "destiny as a woman." As an accident of nature which proved fatal to a woman who had cast her lot with a "femininity" which makes no room for a fully trusting relationship with a husband or with other women, the episode speaks to the self-destructive quality of that myth. Some force in the world—wom-an's own complicit desire for the maternity of the myth, the disorderly energies of sex and the body, the malice of individual and collective men—stands ready to prick a hole in the diaphragm, to close down the freedom of the passage out. To define that force as "life" and condemn the counterforce, the diaphragm, the abortion, as death, is too simple, Piercy's narrative says. In fact, to women in patriarchal culture, "a society we do not control and scarcely influ-ence, [in which] we survive and perish both by taking lovers" (551), the opposite may be true.

*

"With my poems I finally won even my mother. The longest wooing of my life." It is interesting to consider that the mother wooed and won by the poem-producing but childless Jill Stuart is the only one of the protagonists' mothers alive and in good health at the end of these four novels. Maria Wyeth's mother, dead in an "accidental" car crash, surfaces along with Maria's repressed, aborted self as the memory of a figure yearning to "fly the ocean in a silver plane." The mother of the narrator of *Surfacing*, dead years before, returns along with the repressed memory of her aborted self both as the human mother who broke her ankles thinking she could fly from the roof of a barn and as the visionary maternal guide to the experience in the woods which exorcised "the old belief that I am powerless." Felicitas Taylor's mother is included with her daughter in her granddaughter's vatic, final speech-act, "we are not dying," but Felicitas has before this affirmed that her acceptance of her own maternity was precisely the signal that allowed her mother, and the others of that generation of mothers, to begin to grow old and die, since now "They could leave things to me" (257).

The mothers of the protagonists in these novels, in various degrees complicit with patriarchy, powerless and fearful, cannot keep their daughters free or themselves alive. When their daughters become biological mothers they are marked as mortal, but the imaginary child—the ghost children of Didion's and Atwood's abortion protagonists, the haunting Donna, and the other poetic fictions of Piercy's Jill—somehow restores the mother, the original "lover," original home, the "imaginary" itself. The novels that close on an achieved biological motherhood—Maria "playing" for Kate, Felicitas protecting Linda—must accept some element of entrapment in that closing. Like Drabble's Rosamond these mothers are embedded in time, plotted into a game. They must look to an end, begin to die.

The novels that culminate in a meeting with ghosts, strive against closure. In these opened worlds, *Surfacing*'s protagonist still follows her dead mother and father, harboring the mystic "baby in the bottle" of her womb, a kind of third eye. And *Braided Lives*'s Jill still carries the ghost child "Donna" as the undeliverable source for her poems. And *The Middle Ground*'s Kate Armstrong sees in the fairy tale windings of London's rivers and streets the "little sister" who was her mother, her child self and her aborted child, her full being, "always decaying yet always renewed . . . unplanned . . . intricate, enmeshed . . . the old and the new side by side."

3
Abortion and the Fears of the Fathers: Five Male Writers

mpathetic with women characters, deeply conflicted about women's choices, male writers in the twentieth century still resonate most profoundly to the special exposures of the man in the matter of maternal choice. Faulkner's Addie Bundren makes a discovery: she had remained complete and somehow untouched during intercourse, but in her first pregnancy her "aloneness" had been "violated." Pregnancy was rape. But birth made the violation "whole again." It is true that the circle binding the violated mother and child never loses the elementary violence introduced by the father: "Only through the blows of the switch could my blood and their blood flow as one stream." But the primary fact here is the exclusion of the father and the entire apparatus of phallogocentric reality from that circle: "My aloneness had been violated and then made whole again by the violation: time, Anse, love, what you will, outside the circle."[1] "Love," a word which like all words, says Addie, is "just a shape to fill a lack," was the husband's bid for immortality. Instead, the birth of his son spun him out of the circle of life: "And then he died. He did not know he was dead" (166).

Better attuned to the same dark premonition, the father in Hemingway's "Indian Camp" cuts his own throat as an "exalted" Doctor Adams, a successful "fisherman" that day, completes a cesarian delivery, sewing up the mother "with nine-foot, tapered gut leaders."[2] The Indian husband "couldn't stand things," the doctor explains later to the appalled onlooker, his own son, Nick. On the trip home, father rowing the boat, passenger-son trailing his hand in the fertile water, startling a trout into its arcing leap, Nick savors his own immortality, a fragile fiction which lasts only as long as it takes his own father to sense his exclusion, his death, and shoot himself.

The same premonition haunts the male protagonist of Hemingway's famous abortion story, "Hills Like White Elephants," a restless terror that the Australian writer Thomas Keneally will allow the articulate embryo of his 1979 fable, *Passenger,* to state about his father: "He cringed at the possibility of observation by unborn and kingly me."[3] This premonition about the undertow in the stream of progress generates a counterinsight in the protagonist of English writer Graham Swift's powerful historical novel of 1984, *Waterland,* that "however much you resist them, the waters will return; that the land sinks; silt collects; that something in nature wants to go back."[4] Swift's history teacher narrator, Tom Crick, is a critic of the "myth of progress" which his Victorian male ancestors created/believed, not knowing that with each move forward they became just a little more dead. "Reality," "that empty but fillable vessel" (31) whose human form is the womb of woman, must for Tom Crick pay due respect to the "natural" truths of return, going back, stopping altogether. To abortion.

Yet as we shall see, the plot of *Waterland* is conflicted about the abortion it uncovers: three deaths, not one, result from it, along with, thirty-six years later, the madness of the female protagonist and, arguably, of the male narrator, haunted by the truth, vision, or guilty desire for the stopped life.

Behind the primal scene of terrible female choice (abortion) presided over by Swift's witchlike woman healer, lies the primal scene of male control shadowing, forcing that choice—patriarchal incest. A key element, too, in John Irving's 1985 novel about an abortionist, *The Cider House Rules,* father-daughter incest represents the ultimate refusal of the father to be excluded. Incest is at once a powerful standard "justification" for abortion—"It may help you to know who the father is. . . . Her father is the father," an outraged woman tells Irving's morally conflicted male doctor—and an emblem of male control, part of the force opposed to abortion as emblem of female choice.[5] In Swift's narrative these two forces deadlock: life stops; reality runs out; "we trip over empty bottles" is the final grim comment. In Irving's narrative, a loose, baggy imitation of its overtly Victorian ancestor, the incestuous father is vanquished, in pity and irony, by the aborting daughter. Abortion, now seen as fundamental to choice itself, male and female, the doctor's and the woman's, in a patriarchal world, is established as part of the precariously "comic" resolution.

Yet here, too, the exclusion of the father is wryly testified to. Homer Wells must leave his son to the family created around the mother, Candy, and her sterile husband, Wally, in order to take up his responsibility for "the Lord's work": delivering unwanted babies but caring for them in his orphanage, or "delivering mothers" by abortion, if that is the woman's choice. The exclusion is wryly testified to and yet artfully overcome, as I shall argue, in the godlike artifice of the motherless, father-son bond created between the delivering doctors and the orphaned boys (not, emphatically, the girls) of Irving's St. Cloud's Orphanage.

Hemingway and Faulkner: Valorous Birth

T he classic American short story about abortion omits the word. In Ernest Hemingway's "Hills Like White Elephants" a young American man and a girl, waiting at a railroad junction by a river in Spain, make the kind of desultory conversation—the scenery, what to drink—which in Hemingway always builds rather than hides tension. The man remarks on the "awfully simple operation" they are apparently headed for: "It's really not anything. It's just to let the air in" (275). The man fears the coming child: "I don't want anybody but you. I don't want anyone else" (277). He wants the freedom, the "air," the vacuum of their gypsylike lovers' life, which consists, in the girl's bleak view, simply of looking at things and trying new drinks. The man believes that "afterward," they'll be "just like we were before," that time can be stopped, actions erased without payment. "The girl," spokesperson in this story for the Hemingway code, knows better. You always "pay" for sexuality in Hemingway, as you "pay" for anything, good or bad. In this case the girl intuits that the fact of abortion will loom as largely, change as much, in their relationship, as would birth. Her silences, then her questions—"And you think then we'll be alright? . . . If I do it you won't ever worry? (275)—are her way of asking him to probe his denial of the fact she knows. His refusal to do this takes the particularly frustrating form of a reiterated insistence that he will not force her to do it, an insistence that locates all responsibility for birth or abortion, all payment for sexuality, in her. In despair she makes the decision to abort, but his brightly hysterical reiterations—"perfectly simple. . . . I don't want you to do it if you don't want to" (275)— drive her to the very Hemingwayan outburst that is the story's emotional climax: "Would you please please please please please please please stop talking" (277).

Hemingway has located his aborted dialogue in a setting heavy with symbolism: the couple wait at a station between two cities, between the two set of rails, between "the dry side" of the Ebro River Valley and the fertile side, well watered, waving with grain, presided over by hills, as the girl says obliquely, "like white elephants" (273). Something about the phrase annoys the man: the girl's false attempt to be witty and "bright," or the associations of the image itself, a mystic beast he has "never seen." "No, you wouldn't have" (273) the girl notes, quietly accusing. Faintly fabulous, faintly false, an object of desire, an object of ridicule, one man's treasure, another man's junk, the "white elephant" merges with the pregnancy, with the dream of "the whole world" that the lovers seek and are about to lose, because the man will not risk the abridgement of his freedom, the experience of mortality confirmed by a child, the recognition of a world of limits. In the terse dialogue below the man speaks first:

> "We can have everything."
> "No we can't."
> "We can have the whole world."
> "No we can't."
> "We can go everywhere."
> "No we can't. It isn't ours anymore."
> "It's ours."
> "No, it isn't. And once they take it away, you never get it back." (276)

The moral weight of the story is clearly with the girl. Like the young Nick in the earlier story, "The End of Something," she has realized that sexuality/pregnancy means an end to "fun," to life without limits. Braver than Nick or the nameless American of "Hills," she recognizes that pregnancy is the beginning of something else, something worthy, testing, dangerous, fundamental, true. Like *A Farewell to Arms*'s Catherine Barkeley, of whom she seems a preliminary sketch (that novel was begun the following year) she doesn't "care about me" (276). She cares about the Hemingwayan adventure of risk in the world. For a man that risk, holy and deadly, is war; sexuality/pregnancy is a woman's access to that same domain.[6] As Catherine went bravely toward the truth that kills her, as Jig moves toward the abortion that may very well have the same consequence, one senses that Hemingway awards both women the sight of the white elephant while the man sits, free but sightless, outside the circle.

Faulkner's *As I Lay Dying* counterpoints the death and funeral journey of Addie Bundren with the pregnancy and search for abortion of her only daughter, Dewey Dell.[7] Told in a dozen different musing monologues, including that of the coffined but still awesomely present mother, the story locates itself, like all the others in this chapter, near, or in this case for a time, *in,* a river, emblem always of the cycles of natural process, the hidden origins and ends of things. The Bundrens—father, daughter, and four sons—are country people, deeply embedded in earth processes, clownish-looking to the townspeople who try to help them cart the corpse back across the swollen belly of the river to the place of its birth, the town of Jefferson.

The four sons are obsessed with, still half inside, the body of their mother. Cash, the oldest, fashions her coffin so carefully that the artifact itself becomes the body to him. For Jewel, child of Addie's "sin" with Rev. Whitfield, the presence of any other human being in that intimate relationship is unbearable. Taut with rage all his life, he dreams of pre-Oedipal bliss at her death: "It would be just me and her on a high hill, and me rolling the rocks down the hill at their faces" (15). He identifies her with the high-spirited horse she bought him and, in an Oedipal climax, rescues the burning, coffined body from a fire, lifting it, upending it, finally "riding upon it, clinging to it," enclosed with it "in a thin nimbus of fire" (212). The "touched" son, Darl, knows of Addie's decision to die by clairvoyance, sees the body through its long journey into the ground, then topples into madness. The youngest son, Vardaman, identifying the mother with a fish killed for the family dinner the night of her death, watches the coffined body fall into the river during its journey and celebrates the escape, alive, of his mother, the fish. The husband, Anse, outside that circle of obsession, dead to it, stolidly fulfills his wife's last request (buries her in the earth of her origin) and speedily acquires new teeth and a new wife. The resurrections, tragic and visionary, which obsess the boys' visions, are figured comically in Anse's and the novel's last words, "Meet Mrs. Bundren."

But Addie's daughter has no time or room for these obsessions, for her mother's death, or for the misery of the unmilked cow in their barn: "You'll just have to wait. What you got in you ain't nothing to what I got in me, even if you are a woman too" (61), she says. Like "a wet seed wild in the hot blind earth" (61), Dewey Dell is pregnant, beginning to feel that violation her mother spoke of: "I feel my body, my bones and flesh beginning to part and open upon the alone, and the process of coming unalone is terrible" (59). Bound in marriage and ignorance, Addie had submitted to the seed's process, but Dewey Dell's seducer had handed her ten dollars and told her about abortions. Dr. Peabody feels her need driving her gaze through his back—"You could do so much for me if you just would" (50)—but mistakes it for grief over her mother. So Dewey Dell's journey through two towns, across the flooded river and through a burning barn with her mother's body, becomes a search for the means of inhibiting that seed, evading her mother's fate. Ignorantly, she tries two druggists in two towns. The self-righteous Mosely refuses to sell her medicine for that "female trouble," fearing the law, and the unspeakable MacGowan, proposing as cure "the hair of the dog," "the same operation" (237, 239), demands sex as payment for, as sardonic equivalent of, the abortion. The seventeen-year-old victim returns from the "operation" in the cellar bitterly convinced that "it won't work" (242).

MacGowan had given her a nondescript box of capsules and a draught from a bottle he didn't bother to identify (but it smelled like turpentine). If this were some other novelist's world, the draught might well have been turpentine and "worked," stopping the life of fetus and mother alike. But in Faulkner's violent and gravid world, wet seeds always germinate. The fundamental fact of lack, emptiness, nonbeing, which maddens the sensitive and truthful characters like Addie and Darl—the fact which Faulkner sees is only fact in the context of human desire—is filled, overturned, swept away in the uncaring current of being's plenitude. It is easy and classic criticism to see Faulkner's women, Lena Grove and Dewey Dell, as symbols of this mindless plenitude.[8] But for Faulkner, it is really the male who, in terror of exclusion, allies himself with, identifies himself with, the uncaring current of seeds, deeds, words. Addie's outrage at her pregnancy, her attempt to make each succeeding pregnancy "negative" the last, to rid her blood of the encroaching other so that finally, having "given" her children to her husband and each other, she can "get ready to die" (168), suggest that in this story at least, woman is the conscious origin and defender of emptiness.[9] Like Addie's "negativing," Dewey Dell's search for abortion, for a stopping of the river and the wetting of the seed, has a kind of doomed gallantry about it, while male sexuality, ever flowing into Dewey Dell, into "the new Mrs. Bundren" towards expansion and birth, has just a tinge of the ludicrous about it. The novel's most powerful image of this, a French picture in a spyglass that Darl brought home from the First World War of a pig having intercourse with a woman (244), foreshadows a key image of the same stupidly insatiable male sexuality in John Irving's *The Cider House Rules.* But women can't stop the male-abetted flow of plenitude through them when they are alive, violation though it is. Even in her coffin the river reaches for Addie, trying to wet the seed once more, and only the obsessive carpentry of Cash, the bevelled edges tightly fitted to keep her pure for him alone, thwart the process.

Passenger: "You Shall See My Face"

Thomas Keneally's 1979 *Passenger* unites several Hemingwayan and Faulknerian themes—the father's terror and the child's possessive desire of the mother, the alternating and ambiguous tides of male and female desire for and against birth—in a virtuoso fable narrated up to the last pages, the point of birth, by the fetus.[10] His awareness triggered early by a laser beam during a prenatal examination, the novel's protagonist receives in "the duchy of the amnion," through its currents and through the codes of the maternal and paternal DNA, the past history and current doings of his father, an Australian-born journalist named Brian Fitzgerald, and his mother, an Irish-born, would-be novelist named Sal. The story is set in London in 1967, where a doctor in a psychiatric hospital may do a clean legal abortion for sufficient reasons, where journalists catch planes to events in the macrotheater of war—Vietnam, the Sinai Peninsula. Keneally clearly intends the comparison: the body of pregnant Sal is the territory of the microtheater of war where father and son battle for the available quantity of being.

Brian is drawn to both theaters of war by the same magnet—fear. Like Hemingway's heroes, Brian had discovered his mortality in a war experience in the early 1960s in Indonesia. It had left him with "a sort of asthma" which recurs when people like Sal tell him that the unbribable processes of nature are taking him over. The process, for example, by which sons become fathers and at last see that there is no other, buffer generation between them and "the pit" (36). It had also left him with both a taste for, and a distrust of, heroic ideals and behavior, an old yearning for chivalry which is paralyzed by cynicism. Insecure and bereft of ideology, the father-to-be eyes the coming responsibility, and the observing son-to-be comments, "This was yet another reason for his being scared of me. He didn't want me to see him empty-handed" (44).

Brian's fear has made him a persistent womanizer; as he flies off to the Sinai to cover the Egyptian-Israeli War, Sal discovers proof of this. In Israel, surrounded with death, Brian "falls in love" with Annie, another journalist. Returning with her to his already half-abandoned wife and half-consciously feared and hated son-to-be, he proposes full abandonment, divorce, and—as rational "conclusion" to a process which had in fact originated in his terror of fatherhood—abortion. This information understandably shocks the fetus, who had already, we learn, made a "choice" not to be born but rather to live forever in blissful communion with the mother. Brian's choice not to be a father triggers the "passenger's" new choice to be a son. He now "opted for birth, for its puzzles and perils," and joyfully locks in primal combat with the fearful father: "For you shall see my face, you bastard . . . . my ferocious and irrevocable face" (95, 98).

Half-hysterical with anger, her own and the fetus's, the mother makes a poor defender against the male institutions—husband, police, medical establishment—which eventually imprison her in an asylum and prepare her for a "therapeutic" abortion. But Sal and her unborn son have acquired another defender in a mysterious, American thief-businessman called The Gnome, whose poignant obsession with the young Sal as *his* potential mother makes for perhaps the most interesting part of the novel.

The Gnome is a forty-year-old orphan born to a sixteen-year-old mother who had not known she was pregnant. He therefore never sustained the rich and "kingly" psychic interaction, the communications protective, adventurous, and self-awakening, which result in the decision to opt for birth with its puzzles and perils. The man thus has a fundamental perception of himself as not yet born: his years as a man, marked by superficial success, have for him been the doings of a ghost without real power to have opinions, make choices, do deeds. Seeking, like the Christian God, as he sees it, a woman from whom he can at last be born as human, he is attracted by "an aura of rightness" to Sal, identifying her as that "figure from mythology . . . *the good mother*" (102), identifying himself with her fetus, the novel's "passenger."

Though The Gnome is not yet psychically born, the fact that he is physically separated from the consoling river of his mother's blood still makes him suffer to some extent from those walled-in fears which the fetus knows make the separated, born soul "a zoo of vipering doubt" (9). He is not, like Brian, afraid of death. He has been through several harrowing accidents which would have killed him, he thinks, had he been sufficiently "born" to die or even to know about death viscerally. But his alienation from, or rather his lack of introduction to, the world has made him unable to quite take hold of life either. Now, in "communion" with "the good mother," he takes on the decisive qualities of his unborn brother self, the novel's narrator, and lends that puny god strength. He gives the erring husband, the homicidal father, the beating the narrator had wanted to give him and rescues Sal and the fetus from the asylum and the threatened abortion.

In taking them from England to Australia, The Gnome unwittingly parallels the journey Brian's ancestor, an imprisoned political radical, made two hundred years before. Sal's novel in progress is about this ancestor, whose fierce beliefs in human freedom survived defeat in battle, the thousand strokes of the authorities' lash, the humiliation of imprisonment, serfdom, and even the apparent failure of the ideal in his fellow convicts. His conception, intuited by Sal, "that all convict souls, disconnected from each other . . . would in the same instant take fire, get the compulsion, rise up" (171) is "delivered" by the novel in two linked birth/deaths. The Gnome, having performed his deed of rescue, finally falls victim to one of his worldly pursuers, who abandons him in a falling plane.

> The fall was long, but one could see the dazzling and crystalline patterns of the outer world. Born at last, he sang to himself, as the floor struck him and he opted to breathe. But his mouth was filled with an instant and painless fire."
> (75)

And the narrating fetus, taking up with redoubled force after The Gnome's death/birth the responsibility to be born, identifies directly in the moment of his birth, the last moment of his narrative self-consciousness, with the rebel ancestor, Maurice Fitzgerald. As the thousand lashes like "solid fire down on the muscles" (186) become for him the burning lights of the hospital room, "lights that ran molten over my brain" (185), he joins Maurice in the defiant refusal to utter a cry.

At the birth the novel abandons its first person stance: the "neutral gaze" of the child opens "by an act of will" on a "clumsy" father who claims to be a "new man," born into at least a partial understanding of his own fears and the crimes they made him commit, as Sal is a "new woman," delivered by the ordeal of her journey into "a new directness" (188–89). New man or not, the father ends the story outside the circle formed by mother, child, and their new Australian brother-lover-protector, the young, sun-browned surfer with the mythic name of Jason.

Yet the novel's last words are from father to son. The fetus that terrified Brian, godlike in its power to oust him from possession of "the good mother" and leave him facing into the wind of his own mortality, the entity he had wanted to abort and kill, originally had no face: "Only in places like Bangkok did they dare carve gods resembling me—as blunt nosed, intent, detached . . . my hands extended cunningly in front of my mouth" (6). The birth of the passenger is a trauma for all those about him, the fearful born, the half born in need of rebirth. For the fetus himself, it is a matter of abandoning that faceless godhood for an identifiable face, one that breathes the fire of air, the human condition of pain, instead of the waters of paradise, the womb. Interestingly, the narrative underlines this "humanizing" the way *The Millstone* does, by supplying the now human child with a heart defect, a sentimental touch which breaks down the last barriers between son and father, who hurries to the hospital. Apologizing, the ex-aborter greets the ex-god through the glass of the hospital nursery: "You see," he muttered. "It's a matter of being . . . you know . . . presented . . . with people's faces. Yeah. That's what it is" (189).

Waterland: The Stream Flows Backwards

Graham Swift's *Waterland* opens like a Gothic novel with a murdered body floating down the river that drains the English fenland. The narrator is a mysteriously spooked London history teacher whose fenland, paternal forbears were rural lock keepers and tale spinners, and whose maternal forbears were Victorian builders and brewers on the rise, in league with progress. Throughout the novel he addresses as his readers a class of adolescents who have suddenly rebelled against "the grand narrative"—history (74). The young people are spooked, too; they are pierced by nuclear fear, the recognition that the future, which is all that makes the past significant, may be foreclosed. Their challenge to the teacher, Tom Crick, culminates two other disasters. His headmaster, a nononsense technocrat with an airy faith in a future under the nuclear umbrella, has used the excuse of Thatcherite cuts in the budget to eliminate the history department and, by implication, Crick, too. And his wife, Mary, returning in her childless, early fifties to the Roman Catholic religion she had grown up in, began a "love-affair, a liaison . . . with God" (31), whose issue was the kidnapping by the would-be, couldn't-be mother of another woman's baby from the supermarket.

The narrative is carried back from these present errors in rushes, oozes, and broken crosscurrents of self-interrupted musing, explaining, and reasoning, to the three deaths which at some profound level stopped the lives, the stories, of Tom Crick and Mary Metcalf, his wife. For, Crick warns his students in the obscure early pages of his rambling, "there is such a thing as human drainage, too, such a thing as human pumping" (23). And the subsequent "pumping" of Mary and Tom, sexually, socially, intellectually, produces energies which drain continually back to the murder of Freddie Parr, found floating in the lock of the Leem River in 1943, the suicide (if it was such) of the murderer, and the pregnancy/abortion that caused and was caused by these.

Of the three mysteries these deaths involve, the first introduced is the most easily explained and the first illuminated. The narrator's brother, the mentally retarded "potato head," Dick Crick, killed Freddie Parr by getting him drunk on a bottle of his grandfather's famous Coronation Ale, then hitting him on the head and pushing him into the river. He did it because he was, in his dim but intense way, in "lu— lu— love" with Mary Metcalf and believed that desire alone was sufficient to make him the father of the child the sixteen-year-old Mary was carrying. This naive belief runs in the family: brother Tom believed that desire alone is sufficient (and necessary) to fill "that empty but fillable vessel, reality" of which a woman's womb is "a miniature model" (31). Mary's protest, protecting Tom, the real father, that their friend Freddie Parr was the father, thus outraged not only Dick's manhood but his very reality. For Dick is (more than he or we know at the moment) the child of the maternal Atkinson ancestors, a child of "progress" for whom the things that happen, are done, are made, *are* reality. Tom, on the other hand, is a child of their Crick ancestors, rural philosophers like Faulkner's

Bundrens for whom events, deeds, are mere hallucinations in the everlasting flatland of vacancy, for whom "reality is that nothing happens" (30).

The Atkinson vision thus privileges paternity as the ultimate sign of reality: Atkinsons will seek fatherhood, invest it with godhood, be unable to relinquish it. But the Cricks have been "water people" (1) for hundreds of years, living on its animals, sustaining and repairing its ravages, receiving its draining cargoes, and taking to heart its message: "For what is water, children, which seeks to make all things level, which has no taste or colour of its own, but a liquid form of Nothing?" (101). For the Cricks, fatherhood is what it was to primitive peoples, man's hallucination, his favorite fiction, poignant attempt to raise on the flats of reality, in the empty womb of it, "his own personal stage, his own props and scenery—for there are very few of us who can be, for any length of time, merely realistic" (30). A Crick will not believe his own fatherhood nor insist upon it, nor, on the other hand, will he be destroyed by it or by its lack.

This is what Tom Crick claims to understand of his own vision as he looks back beyond and around the conception and abortion of his only child, a primal scene reluctantly uncovered by the skittering narrative as a series of nightmarish snapshots. It started with "curiosity," a "vital force," an "itch," which drove the fifteen-year-old Mary to explore her own and Tom's bodies, an itch "beyond all restraint" (38) whose verbal form, "those spell-binding words which make the empty world seem full," is (as it was in Faulkner's novel) the repeated phrase drained of reality, "I love—I love—love, love" (39). It begins in a "little game of tease and dare" between the aggressive Mary and two boys, Tom Crick and Freddie Parr, as to who will "show" what lies between the legs. Dick Crick, "potato head," several years older and more physically developed, suddenly makes himself a part of the game when Mary agrees to "show" to the boy who swims longest underwater. Experiencing an erection for the first time, Dick dives from the bridge and wins the game, the splash and swim itself serving as his act of intercourse with the river, with Mary, with the fillable vessel of reality. The whimsical and malignant Freddie Parr, seeing Dick, bewildered, fail to claim his trophy, initiates another game: he seizes an eel from the river trap and thrusts it into Mary's "knickers." And Dick, erection, dive, eel, and ejaculation combining in his rudimentary mind, begins a kind of courtship of Mary, bringing her an eel in an act which to him signifies his creativity, his fatherhood, his reality.

So the first fragment of mythic memory—Dick, ready, erect, on the bridge; Freddie in the water reaching for the eel; Mary, "impregnated"—contains all the elements of the second—Freddie, dead in the water from Dick's possessively paternal blow; and Mary, pregnant and, good Catholic girl that she is, "responsible," telling the terrified and shamed actual father, Tom, "I know what I'm going to do" (199). Mary is frozen in guilt, "so inside herself she might never emerge again. And inside Mary who's sitting so inside herself, another little being is sitting there, too" (199).

The abortion Mary plans is both her effort to emerge from herself, from her guilty self-imprisonment, and her effort to expiate one death with another, to punish in herself the sexual curiosity that led to Dick's murder of Freddie. It is a ritual of abasement and sacrifice which Swift's narrative connects with her Roman Catholicism: at the crisis of the abortion, "with a terrible involuntary persistence," comes the phrase from her school prayers, "Holy Mary Mother of God Holy Mary Mother of God Holy Mary Mother of—" (232). Tom is excluded from this decision. It is Mary who first tries abortion by dislodgement: "She jumps. Her skirt billows; brown knees glisten. And she lands in what seems a perversely awkward posture, body still, legs apart, not seeming to cushion her fall but rather to resist it. Then, letting her body sink, she squats on the grass, clasps her arms round her stomach. Then gets up and repeats the whole process. And again. And again" (219–20). Then, miscarriage begun but not completed, Mary makes the ultimate decision: "Little cramps—not so little cramps—in Mary's guts. And Mary says at last, because it's not working, it's not happening: 'We've got to go to Martha Clay's'" (224).

Martha Clay, fen dweller, "witch," living image along with her mate, Bill, of Tom's Crick ancestors, the water people (8), performs the abortion in a nightmarish evocation of the force that empties, drains, the vessel of reality:

A pipe—no, a piece of sedge, a length of hollow reed—is stuck into Mary's hole. The other end is in Martha's mouth. Crouching low, her head between Mary's gory knees, her eyes closed in concentration, Martha is sucking with all her might. Those cheeks—those blood-bag cheeks working like bellows. . . . Martha appears to have just spat something into the pail. . . . In the pail is what the future is made of. I rush out again to be sick. (232)

A figure from Tom's own kind of nightmare, Martha beckons him back into the circle, the decision from which Mary would have excluded him. After the long process of drainage, in the dawn, Martha orders him to empty the pail of "the future" into the water, the liquid form of nothing: "You gotta do it, bor. Only you. No one else. In the river, mind" (238). So his seed is abandoned to the river, as was his brother Dick's in that first dive after his first erection. Tom Crick's vision of reality is sealed by that abortion, draining, flowing back, stopping. The whole superstructure of his subsequent life, love, and marriage with the abortion-injured and now barren Mary, the ever-filling "grand narrative" of history, the precarious "fatherhood" of the teacher with his students, is a gallant fiction extended over that fundamental fact. It collapses, paradoxically, when the fiction becomes intolerable for Mary and she opts for the madness of an alternate vision: that God has offered to her aged womb a child, like the patriarch of the Old Testament did to Sarah, the patriarch of the New Testament to Elizabeth. Though her husband forces her to return the stolen child, as Martha had forced him to look on the reality which is drainage, she will never, Tom knows as he visits her in the "temporary" criminal asylum, submit to emptiness, will always grieve for the baby she believes she bore at age fifty-two, "the baby they took away from her and won't give back. That baby who, as everyone knows, was sent by God. Who will save us all" (247).

With that phrase the story of Tom Crick's aborted fatherhood is linked with the messianic madness, the driven Atkinson pride, that produced empire, fueled war, sired Dick Crick, the mysterious elder brother whose attempts at lu— lu— love were behind the whole tragedy. Behind the tragedy of Dick's mental retardation is the

Atkinson lu— lu— love (poignant, neurotic, incestuous) which begot him—a love timed by the "great narrative of history" to coincide with the Great War in which the Victorian dream of progress, of the March of Mind, of the primacy of energy over matter and of event and deed over reality, circled back upon itself and blew itself up (to quote an American tale of incest and the Great War, Fitzgerald's *Tender Is the Night*) "in a great gust of high explosive love."[11]

The story of the "rise" of the Atkinson side of the narrator's family from Crick-like flatlanders and water people to hillside shepherds, barley farmers, then monopolist brewers, land reclaimers, transportation barons and heads of local government, is a story of "the tenacity of ideas" over/against "the obstinacy of water" (52). It is also a story of powerful but blind patriarchs and haunted and haunting wives, of men who sought to control their women like their water.[12] A blow struck out of psychotic jealousy by Thomas Atkinson in 1820 puts his beautiful wife, Sarah, in a waking coma for the next fifty-four years, and, despite his external activity, internally "history has stopped for him" at that moment, waters leveling once again the "unreclaimable internal land" (60). And while his son and grandson maintain "the driving force of the Atkinson machine" (64) through the century, the traumatized wife mutters or screeches three words, "smoke . . . fire . . . burning" (63) at intervals, dives into the Ouse River "like a mermaid," according to local legend, just before her funeral, and, according to the same source, presides over the conflagration which destroys the Atkinson Brewery in the last moments of the long Edwardian summer, 1911.

Tom Crick possesses the journal of his grandfather (Sarah's great grandson), Ernest Atkinson, in whom the engine of progress finally strips its gears. The journals record Ernest's late Victorian doubts, financial and political failures. They follow his descent into a mysticism in which he brews a hallucinogenic, Coronation Ale, suffers and imposes an incestuous love upon his teenage daughter, Helen, and finally, despairing of humanity as his doubts and Sarah's ghostly prophecies have their culmination in World War, conceives the mad but tenacious idea that only beauty, a child of beauty, his own child begotten of his own Helen, can "become a Saviour of the World" (166).

So Helen Atkinson, like Mary Metcalf thirty years later, becomes a ghostly emblem of Sarah Atkinson, "who, local lore has it, offers her companionship to those whose lives have stopped though they must go on living" (89). Loving her father, seeing his diseased desire, Helen tried first to divert it. She helped him found an asylum for shell-shocked veterans: "Wasn't that a better plan? To rescue all these poor, sad cases, all of whom would be in a sense their wards, their children" (171). But the father was adamant: both his Atkinson desire to control, possess, and materialize in his own deed, the idea, the "Saviour of the World," the son of beauty, and his counter-Atkinson despair at the secret failures of progress, drive him to this incest: "When fathers love daughters and daughters love fathers it's like tying up into a knot the thread that runs into the future, it's like a stream wanting to flow backwards" (172).

The daughter's compromise, to marry the convalescing soldier Henry Crick but bear as his first child her father's projected saviour, frees her for a kind of future and triggers a last visit from the ghost of Sarah Atkinson as well as the suicide of the (next-to) last Atkinson: "Because on the same September evening that my father saw a will o' the wisp come twinkling down the Leem, Ernest Atkinson, whose great-grandfather brought the magic barley down from Norfolk, sat down with his back against a tree, put the muzzle of a loaded shotgun into his mouth and pulled the trigger" (177).

The child of incest, "Saviour of the World," is Dick Crick, "potato head." This last Atkinson grows up like a Crick, deft handed, water drawn, apparently vacant brained. But as his brother, the narrator, noted, none of us, however apparently well-fitted for it, can be truly realistic—empty—all the time. In Dick's brain the disappearance (death) of his mother, Helen, becomes linked with his (putative) father's trips to the eel traps in the river, as well as with the substance (Ernest's last cache of Coronation Ale) in the bottles his grandfather (who was really his father) left him in the chest with the journals that he couldn't read, though his brother Tom could. Out of this draught of his heritage, together with the sexual play with Mary

117

and the eel which he witnessed and then took part in, Dick constructs a myth, incestuous in its turn, Oedipal, of a mother who will "rise up, wriggling and jiggling, alive—alive—o, out of the river" (185); who may consummate his earliest desire if he dives with force into the river, refuses to relinquish that desire. When he goes to the river after Tom's guilty and desperate revelation of his incestuous origin he is, Tom speculates, partly feeling that counter-Atkinson despair at the botch, the emptiness he is. But his dive has the look not of self-immolation but of search, another Atkinson push toward the idea, another gallant, if futile, move into the future which is, in reality, governed by the backward flow of the liquid form of nothing. It is a dive which kills him.

The Cider House Rules: Doctor's Choice

Like almost all the texts studied here, including those written after the Supreme Court decision of 1973, John Irving's *The Cider House Rules* is set in prelegalization days. But it alone takes up at length the issue *Roe vs. Wade* made key in America: the "choice" is an affair "between a woman and her doctor." Since men have taken over the medical establishment of the West from midwives, a second male role, a final "fatherhood," enters the arena of maternal choice. Irving's doctors have no choice, of course, under the law, so it is as outlaws, like the women, that they enter into moral debate over whether abortion is "the Lord's work" or "the Devil's work," as Dr. Wilbur Larch hears it phrased.

The older doctor, Larch, made his decision in the early part of the century after witnessing the horrors of women's self-induced or non-medical abortions. He will abide by the woman's choice: "He would deliver babies. He would deliver mothers, too" (67). The younger man, Homer Wells, has a much harder time. His anonymous mother made the choice to bear him and allow the delivering Dr. Larch to keep him at his orphanage; neither he nor Dr. Larch know why her choice set him where he is, rather than in the orphanage's leak-proof disposal basket, ready for the incinerator. So precarious an origin plays its part in orphaned Homer's respect for life. Yet in the end Homer accepts the responsibility to be a servant to woman's choice, too. Paradoxically, he comes to believe, as long as women have no legal right to a safe abortion, the doctors who have those skills have no moral right to withhold them. Only when an individual woman may choose, if she wishes, a safe, legal abortion from doctors willing to perform them, may an individual doctor who is morally opposed, choose to withhold that service, knowing that another individual doctor may choose to give it.

The novel is set in Maine in roughly the 1920s through the 1950s. One of its conceits is to omit the final digit of any date, as if to indicate awareness that in showing debate about the issue of abortion it is handling matters which may reach a court of law and therefore needs to disguise its facts. In an orphanage in a town ruthlessly built and callously abandoned by the proprietors of the Ramses Paper Company, Dr. Wilbur Larch, Harvard Medical School graduate, receives the desperate women who made the choice to deliver, or be delivered from, what his moral choice tells him is "the product of conception." In his teens Wilbur Larch had one sexual experience (a whore, Mrs. Eames, was a "present" from his father) which resulted in gonorrhea, an ether addiction, and a personal choice of sexual abstinence. Later, during his medical residence in Boston, he saw Mrs. Eames die horribly mutilated from a self-induced abortifacient. Refusing Mrs. Eames's prostitute daughter the illegal but safer abortion she asked him for the next day, he had to watch her die, too, of the quack-abortionist method that had been used on her. Mrs. Eames's daughter, who had been present during Larch's sexual initiation, pinned an accusatory note to her dress before she went to the quack. It said, "Dr. Larch—Shit or get off the Pot!" (50). She turns up several years later in a pornographic photograph, suffering oral sex with a pony. Incredibly tough, but victimized and dead through the Harvard doctor's choice, Mrs. Eames's daughter becomes the novel's emblem of female suffering. Stung, the young Dr. Larch visits the quack-abortionist and carries off the current client, a thirteen-year-old girl raped by her father, to perform his first illegal abortion.

Thus from the novel's beginning the skill of the doctor figures, ambiguously and obscurely tragic, both as sublimation/reparation of his own sexuality and as a kind of fatherhood as disturbing as it is healing. The doctor's speculum and curettes function to undo (or is it to redo?) the incestuous violence of male sexuality: "About a third of them get it from their fathers, or their brothers. Rape. Incest. You understand?" says the quack-abortionist.

And caught between, fillable vessel of reality, is the woman. As Mrs. Eames's daughter, mouth filled with pony penis, body distended with pregnancy and then with abortifacient, is the emblem of female suffering, the orphan called Melony (a typing mistake for Melody) is Irving's memorable figure of female rage at this trap. A Victorian to the core (he wanted "to be—as he put it—'of use' " [7]), Dr. Larch reads *David Copperfield* at night to the boys' division of the orphanage and *Jane Eyre* to the girls ("What in hell else would you read to an orphan?" [26]). The sixteen-year-old Melony, solidly built and powerful, the opposite of Mrs. Eames's wiry daughter or frail Jane, shouts in scorn against Jane's tenderer feelings, not at first recognizing her foremother. But like the young Jane and the older alter-ego, Bertha Mason Rochester, "Melony was always angry" (82). The "undisputed heavyweight of the girls' division" (84), Melony shows "only the top of the iceberg" of her anger when she objects to the passage in which the orphaned and enraged Jane admits that the songs of the motherly servant, Bessie, provided some "gleams of sunshine . . . even for me" (77). Her rage makes her unadoptable. When she herself "adopts" the fourteen-year-old Homer as her "sunshine," it is in scorn of him *and* sunshine *and* adoption.

In her favorite place, an abandoned, half-destroyed wooden building whose destruction she methodically completes, she offers the paradoxical rationale of their relationship: " 'Sunshine,' Melony said, finding a small pane of glass that hadn't been smashed—and smashing it—'Sunshine, we've got *nobody*. If you tell me we've got each other, I'll kill you' " (89). In this, Irving's revision of the "red room scene" in Bronte's novel, Melony throws a snake to a hungry hawk, demolishes the building, swears to find her mother and kill her, too. Whether for bearing her, abusing her, or abandoning her is uncertain and immaterial; it is the human, especially female, condition that enrages Melony. Her failure to engage the equally orphaned Homer Wells in this same existential anger enrages her still more: "Why aren't you angry? What's wrong with you? You're never going to find out who did this to you!" (98). Like

Jane Eyre's anger, Melony's burns itself out in the red rooms of the orphanage and eventually the world without providing real satisfaction: watching the destroyed building float away in fragments, "'Neat, huh!' Melony asked dully" (99). Like Bertha Mason Rochester's anger, however, it tirelessly renews itself against targets human and inanimate, innocent and guilty, all loved/hated like the fact of existence itself.

Both Homer and Melony freeze with recognition at Jane Eyre's observation that "it is in vain to say human beings ought to be satisfied with tranquility: they must have action, and they will make it if they cannot find it" (125). But Homer's anger and grief at his orphaned situation, sublimated like his deliverer-father's in the Victorian desire to be "of use," will seek action like Jane's in work, while Melony's work, through two decades of Jane Eyre-like self-support in the fields and factories of Maine, is a mere pedestal for the awesome and unchanging figure of her rage. When Homer deserts the orphanage in young manhood in search of his own kind of action, Melony agonizes like Jane over the absence of Rochester, but Jane's self-disciplined decision to do without him contains no help for Melony. She abandons the book and sets out after Homer, whether to kiss or kill him she hardly knows herself. Though she finds a substitute lover in a woman, Lorna, Melony "wondered where her rage would go" (424) if she settled down with her. That rage, established with black-comic authority during the novel's first chapters, stalks the edenic landscape of apple orchards and cider houses where Homer Wells makes his action. That rage is part of this novel's "undertoad": a term Irving coined in *The World According to Garp* (1978) to describe the violence and malevolence loose in the world, which collect during the narrative, obscurely but surely carrying catastrophe toward its hero.

Where the self-originated violence of *Jane Eyre* marks Melony's story, Homer Wells's key text is *David Copperfield*, especially the opening sentence, which has, to himself at thirteen and to the younger male orphans he reads it to, "the effect of a litany": "Whether I shall turn out to be the hero of my own life, or whether that station will be held by anybody else, these pages must show" (71). In Dickens's narrative, of course, violence and malevolence are displaced external to "the hero": the world acts—beats him, exiles and imprisons him, enchants and betrays him—and he reacts. This is why he doubts his heroism, his centrality to his own story, until the act of storytelling, novel writing, makes him so—the only thing that could.

Homer gets this reading assignment at the initiating age of thirteen. It supplies a text to help pose the question he half understood at his real initiation into the moral and psychic life just before this, when he found on the orphanage grounds a three-month-old fetus, translucent, clearly human, but "nonheroic," and heard from Dr. Larch the full explanation of his work at St. Cloud's Orphanage. The mothers Homer has seen coming to the door may either have their baby or—"kill it," Homer supplies. "Stop it," Larch counters, "an orphan or an abortion" (74). Stunned by the precariousness of existence—how much distance really separates an orphan from an abortion?—Homer shrinks from all action except a trembling and undifferentiated, propitiating human kindness. He easily resists Melony's invitation to violence (though not her sexual initiation), but other forces are gathering. The aging Dr. Larch dreams that Homer might follow him as delivering doctor-father to orphans (or abortions) and begins teaching him gynecological and pediatric medical procedure. But in a key encounter when he is twenty, Homer holds another fetus in his hand: Dr. Larch had asked him to autopsy the unborn baby of a woman knifed to death. And in this moment he intuits the presence in the fetus of a soul, a potential "hero."

This moment of profound separation from his doctor-father coincides with the arrival at the orphanage of the couple who will be L'il Emily and Steerforth to his David (except when he plays Steerforth in the erotic triangle), a beautiful, healthy, and sweet-natured couple from orchard country named Candy Kendall and Wally Worthington, who have come for an abortion. Raised in loving homes, secure in a future as an engaged couple, heirs to thriving apple orchards, the blond Candy and Wally dispense sweet and easy love and comfort to the angst-ridden occupants of the orphanage. Candy's abortion seems to them a sensible response to a small problem in the timing of their first child. "No veiled future glanced upon him in the moonbeam" (200), Homer quotes David of Steerforth as he accompanies the handsome and generous Wally back to the orchard to pick up some trees to bring back to the orphanage. But the allusion has set up tremors in the narrative analogous to those tremors in Dickens's narrative that foreshadow "the Tempest" of Steerforth's betrayal of David with his protégée, Emily.

In Irving's novel, however, amid the apples of Ocean View Orchard, it is Homer who has to fall into the corrupt action of illicit love and Wally over whom the tempest of violence rolling towards Homer in the narrative will break instead. World War II delights the active Wally with its heroic possibilities; the reactive Homer decides innocently to stay at the orchard. He is enabled to do this, interestingly, because Dr. Larch, a fiction maker like Margaret Drabble and Thomas Keneally, decided, like them, to give his precious child a humanizing flaw, a heart defect. Since he controlled the records of all births at St. Cloud's Orphanage he easily could insert the protecting notation which makes Homer 4-F.

Homer and Candy fall in love while Wally is away and conceive a child, which Dr. Larch delivers and Homer "adopts." Wally returns after much heroic suffering, a cripple and sterile. The casual abortion that brought them originally to St. Cloud's in fact terminated Wally's first and last possibility of biological fatherhood. The tense and guilty love, which Candy and Homer maintain during the war years and for fifteen years after Candy helplessly marries the returned hero, gave Homer a blood fatherhood he can never claim.

Both these pregnancies were unplanned: they happened in spite of prophylactic precaution, because the intelligent and honorable mothers and fathers wanted neither an orphan nor an abortion. The pregnancy and birth of Homer and Candy's "Angel" comes from the force in human affairs called error, ignorance, mistake—a mistake by Homer in the use of the condom. But the earlier pregnancy of Candy and Wally that ended with the choice of abortion was the result of a sterner force, a directed malevolence allied with "the undertoad" that Irving captures in an unsettling encounter between Homer Wells and the shallow Lothario of the orchards, Herb Fowler.

Fowler has the macho habit of handing out condoms to all the men of his acquaintance as he urges them to duplicate his own inexhaustible sexual performance. Learning from Wally that he had used one of Herb's "protections" during the period Candy became pregnant, but that it had had a hole in it, Homer examines his own "present" from Herb and finds an identical hole, "tiny but precise . . . deliberate . . . perfectly placed dead center" (303). A vision of pure evil makes Homer shiver, a vision of bruised women and dead fetuses, their hands curled beseechingly, accusingly. It is a vision of an evil beyond, more mysterious than, sexual exploitation. An evil which makes "rules" for sex without pregnancy and then undermines those rules. An evil not avoiding but seeking the production of orphans and abortions, and of the dead or despairing women who are forced by the perfectly placed pinprick in the condom to choose one or the other.[13]

As the novel moves past midpoint and its Homeric hero travels away from the orphanage, the discourse of "rules" becomes key, replacing the discourse of law which, as developed around the abortion issue at the orphanage, had been dismissed as unworkable. When Homer comes with Wally and Candy to Ocean View Orchards, first to visit, finally to live and work, he notices a list of "Cider House Rules" posted for the workers, especially the migrant workers, mostly black, who are new to the business each year. "The Rules" make a rough and kindly sort of sense: don't operate the grinder if you've been drinking; don't go into the cold storage room to sleep.

Unlike "the law," "the rules" allow for human peculiarities. For instance, the Cider House roof, a place of coolness and relative freedom, a place for dreaming and fantasizing about the ocean which can be seen from its height, is a favorite, though dangerous, roost. Wally's mother, the owner, would prefer to avoid that danger and the expensive repairs to the roof made necessary by the practice, but makes no "law" against this activity, only "rules"—don't go up when drinking, don't crowd each other off—for safety. The trouble is, human behavior eludes not only "laws" but "rules," too, especially somebody else's rules. "Nobody pays no attention to them rules" (283); many of the workers can't even read them, yet Olive

Worthington and Homer, when be becomes manager, gallantly and foolishly post them year after year.

Like the "drive-in rules" about "how far you go with a girl" (302) that Homer discovered from Debra Pettigrew on his first post-orphanage date, the Cider House Rules speak poignantly with double tongues about the human desire for order/disorder. Rules are really "private contracts" (456) traceable to a single individual with the charism, "good" or "evil," to define and enforce them. The key rules are always the unwritten and even unspoken ones. And even these rules come inevitably equipped, like Herb Fowler's condoms, with a manufacturer's defect, a hole in the middle through which human behavior, intransigent, escapes even its own desired boundaries.

The real Cider House Rules, Homer learns during his first year at Ocean View Orchards, are Mr. Rose's (379). The picker's crew boss is a smooth, slender, hardworking, utterly self-confident Carolina black man who controls the pickers, and thus the Cider House, with quiet grace. His movements are so quick they seem invisible and make him apparently slow. His pride is so absolute it can afford the appearance of shy humility; his personality exerts force without effort. And he carries a knife. Like his opposite emblem of violence, the bludgeoning Melony, like his fellow outlaw and personal rule maker, Dr. Larch, he is "in the knife business," and, the cowed but admiring pickers advise Homer Wells, "you don't wanna go in the knife business with Mistuh Rose" (323). He can make a man strip naked and dive into a thousand-pound vat of cider to retrieve a carelessly dropped bit of cigarette. He can with quick thumb and forefinger catch someone's tongue in the act of speaking. And his key rule is that when personal violence must be done, the "law" must never know: "We cut each other only so bad that you never see—you never know we was cut" (455).

In the fifteenth year of Homer's management of Ocean View Orchards—the fifteenth year of his private contract of rules as Candy's secret lover, Wally's secret betrayer, Angel's secret biological father—the two sources of violence in the novel, Melony and Mr. Rose, combine to precipitate the crisis, the moment when the novel's David must become the hero of his own life, find and move to its center, choose his destiny. The powerful female orphan, rage intact, finally tracks him down and offers a brutal assessment of his unheroic posture: "ballin' a poor cripple's wife . . . ordinary middle-class shit—bein' unfaithful and lyin' to the kids" (497). Melony's rage brings her, equipped with deadly self-made knife, to the brink of murder, but her disappointment levels the rage to grief, and she leaves. The "one hundred and seventy-five pounds [Melony's weight] of truth [which] struck him in the face and neck and chest" (498) shatter Homer's composure and his compromising contract of rules, though. "I love you, but we're becoming bad people," he tells Candy. "We're doing the wrong thing; it's time to do everything right" (501).

The arrival shortly after of Mr. Rose, demonstrating in a new and terrifying way "the extreme control he had of his world" (525), offers the path to right action in a chapter entitled, finally, "Breaking the Rules." For on this trip Mr. Rose brings along a seventeen-year-old daughter whose name is Rose, who has a baby daughter whose name will be Rose. Mr. Rose, the knife-wielding controller, has eliminated his daughter's boyfriend; any subsequent children of his child, including the one she is now trying to abort, will be his, as she is his.

Rose Rose's smile is missing an eye tooth, clear sign of an elegantly used and almost invisible knife. When Homer's son, Angel, falls in love with her he sees other marks on her body of a skilled and deadly knife demonstrating extreme control of its world. When he tries to teach her to ride a bicycle she falls off every time, roughly jouncing her lower body, clearly trying to do herself an injury, bring about a miscarriage, in a tragically ancient female gesture like that used by Mary Metcalf in *Waterland*. And when Candy, dimly apprehending, climbs, against the rules, to the Cider House roof at an opportune moment, the victimized cry coming from the bed inside, at first indistinguishable from that of a baby, tells her the full tale.

The incestuous father at first seeks common cause with the adulterous pair, fellow rule makers and lawbreakers. But Homer has just received a bitter telegram from Melony: "Dear Sunshine. I thought you was going to be a hero. My mistake. Sorry for hard time" (545). He has also just sustained a grief-stricken accusation over the phone from the abandoned staff at St. Cloud's Orphanage. Dr. Larch has just died; there will be no more deliveries of babies or of mothers, orphans or abortions: "If you know someone who needs it, you'll have to do it yourself" (560).

Once again the extremity of the situation of pregnancy by incest reveals the choicelessness of woman and exposes both the complicity and, somehow, the exclusion of the biological father. Once again, the narrative asserts, the (male) doctor must join the woman in choicelessness, must reverse the tyranny of the (first) father by forcing aside his own moral scruples to make way for the woman's choice. Though for Homer his teenage intuition that every fetus is a soul still holds and makes his decision a personal agony, the cry of the raped daughter for escape from the "rule" of the father causes him to turn his mind to the opening passage of *David Copperfield*. And "Homer Wells made up his mind to be a hero" (562).

The abortion he offers to Rose Rose breaks Mr. Rose's grip on his own tongue, too, and on Candy's. They have drifted long enough: with the story, the truth about the past, that Homer tells Angel and Candy tells Wally, they take the action, the responsibility, for their lives, their flaws, and their rules. They become hero and heroine, protagonists of their own lives. And they must separate.

The stories, the actions, bring pain and ultimately death. But the death by knife that rode on Dr. Larch's curette and that hovered over Homer and Candy through the whole novel, from Melony, from Mr. Rose, strikes not them but the incestuous father. For he has taught his daughter his own brand of control, and after the abortion she moves to take her life into her own hands, too. Her knife cuts her father "so bad" that nobody knows he's cut till his body runs dry of blood. Crazily proud of the keen and subtle stroke that killed him, Mr. Rose stands by the Cider House he ruled until he can stand no more, sits till he drops over from the carefully placed cut, telling the suddenly enlightened and appalled observers the story they must tell the "law," that he had loved the runaway daughter so much that he had killed himself. In the strictest sense, that is true.

The storytelling impulse, filling the vessel of empty reality, is linked to fatherhood here (and in Barth's novels, too) as it was in Swift's *Waterland*. In *Waterland*, the impulse, poignant but doomed, drained, left the arms of mother and lovers empty; here reality makes good the story in a bittersweet turn of the screw for the hero of his own life. For three factors were crucial to Homer's decision to perform the abortion: Melony's visit, Mr. Rose's incest, and the arrival from St. Cloud's Orphanage of an ancient, recently refurbished, doctor's bag bearing the initials F. S., initials of a man who exists only as a fiction. Homer's decision to become that man, inhabit that fiction, means leaving behind the lovely patchwork of rules and roles, deceits and desires (Candy, Angel: now we know the reason for those rose-tinted and insubstantial names), which have served him as reality for more than fifteen years. But it also means taking up the sonship—fictive, motherless, profound—which seems so to haunt the male imagination. "You are my work of art," Dr. Larch writes Homer. "Everything else has been just a job. . . . You are the doctor" (518).

What Larch means here by "the doctor" is not just that responsibility to exercise no "choice" about performing births or abortions until freedom, a seamless thing, belongs both to mothers and to doctors. He means that profounder and more dangerous responsibility to "play God," which is the lot of "the doctor" and of every human who would become the hero, the performer, of his own life, rather than let anyone else (even God) hold that station. Homer has shrunk from this all his life; it is, up to a point, a renunciation the narrative admires. But ultimately this shrinking is, for Irving, unhuman, a condition like that of Keneally's Gnome, actually "unborn."

An identity has been constructed for Homer's new "birth" with the strangely evocative name of Fuzzy Stone. An asthmatic and frail orphan who died at St. Cloud's despite Dr. Larch's best efforts, Fuzzy has been linked to both the key images of victimization in the novel. He looked in terror at the picture of the botched-abortion-killed prostitute with the pony's penis in her mouth: " 'How could she *breathe?*' Fuzzy asked breathlessly. He was wheezing badly when Homer left him" (102). And he also represents the endangered fetus: "Fuzzy Stone looked like a walking, talking fetus. That was what was peculiar about the way you could almost see through Fuzzy's skin and his slightly caved-in shape" (110). To save the other orphans distress, Dr. Larch had never told them Fuzzy died. Instead he created for him a successful adoption. To save St. Cloud's work, legal and "illegal," from the reforming hands of state officials after his death, Dr. Larch created an elaborate fiction of a Fuzzy Stone who grew up to become a Harvard-educated doctor, an obstetrician and pediatrician, and an avowed anti-abortionist: "What a good story! . . . Only one problem," thought Wilbur Larch, dreaming with the stars. "How do I get Homer to play the part?" (269).

Melony and Mr. Rose bring him to play the part he was born to. The "kisses seeking Homer Wells" (422) which Wilbur Larch gave to the other orphans in the boys' division but, paralyzed by his love, was unable to give to Homer, kisses which signify the emotional side of his non-biological fatherhood as the doctor's bag bearing the new initials F. S. signify his aesthetic fatherhood, finally land on the brow of "Dr. Fuzzy Stone." At the end, Fuzzy/Homer takes up Dr. Larch's position as law-abiding but private rule-making head of St. Cloud's Orphanage, secret "deliverer" of its babies and its mothers, and womanless father, in his turn, to its orphans.

*

You are my work of art . . . you are the doctor." Excluded from the maternal scene as "the father," man comes back to take control as "the doctor." This recapitulates the history of medicine: the process climaxes, for American women, with the legal description of the scene of maternal choice as one inhabited not by women alone, but by "a woman and her doctor." But whose doctor is he? Is he the mother's instrument? The father's? The state's? For the protagonists of Joan Didion, Margaret Atwood, Marge Piercy, and, as we shall see, Alice Walker's *Meridian,* the doctor is the law of the father, ultimately of the rapist: he is a predator, and would be, in Atwood's world of mechanizing, death-loving "Americans," even if the so-called mutual decision were birth rather than abortion.

Hemingway's "Indian Camp" brilliantly articulates the dilemma of the male doctor-father. In this story, "nature" has brought the pregnant Indian woman close to death after two days of screaming pain. The excluded Indian father has stretched himself out in the bunk above his wife, knife in hand; the included white doctor intervenes, knife in hand, to perform the victory of art over nature. The red man kills himself because "he couldn't stand things"; so, several stories later, does the white man. Apparently the burdens of manhood are too heavy even when, especially when, the roles of husband and father are augmented by that of "the doctor."

Relieving the male of that burden is clearly the job of the sinister doctor of Barth's *The End of the Road*. Though he appears to practice a "remobilization" therapy based on the necessity of choice, action, he treats his patients by immobilizing them in their chairs for his lectures on their "progress." His prescription is for blind action without engagement or outcome. And when Jake Horner, breaking the rules, involves himself with Rennie, the doctor promises to do the abortion at the price of Jake's permanent immobilization—castration. He winds up doing all the heavy lifting at the doctor's clinic-farm under the direction of the real power behind the throne, the matron, Mrs. Dockey.

John Irving's Dr. Larch was shocked out of his sexuality and fertility by the quickly narrated series of events beginning with his first act of intercourse and culminating in the death of the prostitute's watching daughter from the effect of a clumsy abortion which he, as the doctor, could have prevented by breaking the law to offer her a medically safe choice. Dr. Larch died some sixty years later, in an ether-aided daydream of intercourse with a lusty, French prostitute, suffering respiratory failure in the purely mental encounter with female passion. His fictive son and work of art, "Dr. Fuzzy Stone," gives up fifteen years of blissful if outlaw sexuality as Homer Wells, partly to expiate that outlaw sexuality and ward off its death-dealing curse and partly to join in desexed humility the procession of haggard young mothers who walk the hill to St. Cloud's, and to make sure they find in him the choice of "deliveries" they seek at the top of the hill.

Beyond this, we sense the same bargain with the reality of male exclusion from primary processes that Barth had made. "Fuzzy Stone" is a therapeutic script to remobilize Homer, rescue him from what comes to seem the fool's paradise, the somehow forbidden fruit of physical love and biological fatherhood. His children will be both the women he saves from death by unsafe abortion and the orphans whose mothers choose to deliver and leave at his door. We are not surprised to find that Homer's biological son has become the inevitable and triumphant third term in this procession of male makers—not the father, not the doctor, but the novelist. Perhaps he is even the novelist of *this* novel, Homer's lost child now the creator-deliverer of his own father, the doctor.

4

Black Maternity: "A Need for Someone to Want the Black Baby to Live"

After the eighteenth century, when British laws against the slave trade and other factors slowed the importation of black men and women into the American south to work the fields, keep the houses, and raise the children of the white planter aristocracy, a new kind of marketable commodity began to be even more consciously sown and harvested there—black babies. Though historians are still arguing about the extent to which American practices differed from the outright for profit human breeding enterprises of the Caribbean, there can be little doubt, as Herbert Gutman notes, that in America "the essential value of (black) adult women rested on their capacity to reproduce the labor force."[1] Black maternity in America begins in schizophrenic conflict with itself. On the one hand the fertile woman, often suffering enforced pregnancy, might well turn against her own fertility to take advantage of folkway abortion techniques (see Gutman, 80–82); on the other hand, steady bearing increased the likelihood that the slave woman would not be sold away from her parents' home and that a family, always fragile, always in danger, could be created.

It could be argued that the power of the white master to enforce pregnancy and birth on his black female slaves and market the product of birth is only one Victorian practice of a universal, patriarchal model. But the legal-cultural support of such a system, with whatever uneasiness, for several of the formative generations of the American national psyche, makes it a very special example indeed.

The black baby—as market commodity, as evidence of white-demonized black sexuality, as witness/evidence to racial holocaust, as a beleaguered race's living grasp of its future—is a highly charged site of meanings. Black maternity, encumbered with vassalage, subversive with vengeful witness, divinized, degraded, sweet with promise, suspicious of itself, comes to consciousness in a powerful and conflicted body of writing by contemporary American black women for whom the free black baby is the ultimate example of a dream deferred, a fertility appropriated, hauntingly incomplete.

Gayle Jones's Ursa Corregidora, last of a line of women sired incestuously upon his black daughters by the Portuguese sea captain-slave breeder whose name still brands them, has inherited a maternal mission: "Ursa, you got to make generations. . . . They didn't want to leave no evidence of what they done—so it couldn't be held against them. And I'm leaving evidence. . . . And when it come time to hold up the evidence, we got to have evidence to hold up."[2] Barren because of an injury inflicted by her husband, Ursa transfers her maternity as evidence to another field of witness, the blues songs in which a race's, a gender's, agony survives to be held up: "Then let me give witness the only way I can. I'll make a foetus out of grounds of coffee to rub inside my eyes when it's time to give witness, I'll make a foetus out of grounds of coffee. I'll stain their hands" (54).

Yet this driven maternity, contrived to subvert a genocidal impulse, can carry a homicidal crosscurrent: icon of the father's (white master, castrated black male) possession of the victim mother, who can will unmixedly that the black baby live? "I felt a need for someone to want the black baby to live," says Toni Morrison's Claudia MacTeer, planting marigold seeds in the alien earth of Lorain, Ohio, in a childish invocation to the forces of life.[3] But Pecola's black baby is born dead. Claudia's elliptical expression—wanted somebody to want—testifies to the divisions within, to the Armaggedon of, black maternal instinct. But it suggests as well the absent but prophetically immanent and emphatically collective someone whose desire for the birth of the black baby can overcome the division.

This essay will concentrate on plots of maternal choice and black maternity in several poems, plays, and novels by black women writers. In all of them abortion (birth, too, sometimes) is a matter of extreme woe, often a savage scene of pain, one tired choice in a spectrum of victimizations. Ntozake Shange's Lady in Blue, "pregnant & shamed of myself," makes the grim choice and suffers "eyes crawling up on me / eyes rollin in my things / metal horses gnawin my womb / dead mice fall from my mouth."[4] Alice Walker's novelistic heroine, Meridian, conceives after a wearying, nonorgasmic encounter with her white-woman-obsessed lover, because he had not worn a condom for this casual lovemaking with a black woman. She went for an abortion on her own. The college doctor "tore into her body without giving her anesthesia," deliberately rested his heavy elbow on her navel so that "a whirling hot pain shot from her uterus to her toes," and made a brutal proposition: "I could tie your tubes . . . if you'll let me in on some of all this extracurricular activity."[5]

Yet Walker speaks of her own abortion (when she was the same age as her fictional protagonist), that "secret scary thing," as inseparable from her own dream of actualization. Broke, solitary, sick, "at the mercy of everything, including my own body," Walker said in a 1973 interview, she practiced making razor cuts deep enough to kill herself until "on the last day for miracles" a woman friend found her an abortionist. The scene she depicts here has beauty, not savagery, birth, not death:

> I went to see the doctor and he put me to sleep. When I woke up, my friend was standing over me holding a red rose. She was a blonde, gray-eyed girl, who loved horses and tennis, and she said nothing as she handed me back my life. . . . That week I wrote without stopping . . . almost all the poems in *Once*.[6]

The connection between the choices of abortion and suicide, between that choice and the life of art, can be (has been) appropriately made by women of all colors, notably in *Braided Lives*. What makes this scene of difficult beauty not only "womanist," to use Walker's term, but especially black womanist, is Walker's acute sensitivity, in this and other sections of *In Search of Our Mothers' Gardens*, to the rising rate of suicide among young women of color. They bear the burden of two myths. One, applicable to all politically engaged people of color, is that it is " 'incorrect' to even think of suicide if you are a black person" (271): martyrdom is the "correct" response. The other is the myth of the black earth mother, indestructible under the heaviest load. "I've been hacking away at that stereotype for years, and so have a good many other black women writers," Walker protested in a letter refusing an endorsement to Michelle Wallace's *Black Macho and the Myth of the Superwoman*.[7] But the image dies hard in a black community still depending on it. Or rather, Walker argues, young women of color die of that image. For the black community "could take the black woman as invincible . . . but there was no sympathy for struggle that ended in defeat. Which meant that there was no sympathy for struggle itself—only for 'winning' " (317). From that perspective, it seems that, for Walker, to have the power to abort, to have one's own life given back, is essential to prevent the beleaguered black woman from sinking under the burdens of the maternal myth, black supermom, she carries. At the same time, the sorrow of the imposed choice, even when abortion is available, even when, like Meridian, the woman may give away her child to a decent home elsewhere, makes it clear that women are still in the struggle, not winning.

Walker told the story of Meridian, a Movement voting rights activist of the 1960s for whom there is no victory, only continuing struggle, in 1976. The novel ends with a prison visit to "the child who murdered her child" (211), a teenage infanticide whose act of murder was a kind of suicide: "It was my heart I bit. I strangled it till it died. . . . Where I am, no one is. And why am I alive without my heart?" (212). Meridian herself had borne a child in high school and suffered murderous fantasies about him, which she eventually transferred to herself. Frightened by this narrowing down of choice—infanticide/abortion or suicide—she found a third way. She gave her child out for adoption. But the specially mythicized maternity of her race troubled her dreams for several years.

> Meridian knew that enslaved women had been made miserable by the sale of their children . . . that the daughters of these enslaved women had thought their greatest blessing from 'Freedom' was that it meant they could keep their own children. And what had Meridian Hill done with *her* precious child? . . . A voice (within) cursed her existence—an existence that could not live up to the standard of motherhood that had gone before. (91)

This self-hating voice, which marks what the narrator calls Meridian's "spiritual degeneration," changes in the novel's finale to speak not exactly of healing but of a call to healing. Still unable to "rouse her own heart to compassion for her [own] son," Meridian warms to the imprisoned infanticide teenager, "the child who killed her child," and begins the process of self-forgiveness. At novel's end she disappears into the world of struggle without "winning," having survived and passed on to black woman and man alike a stronger birth, a more intense maternity. Her place in the visible community is taken by her black male lover, Trueman, who wonders, in a rhetoric which restores the double meaning to the word *bear*, "if Meridian knew that the sentence of bearing the conflict in her own soul which she had imposed on herself—and lived through—must now be borne in terror by all the rest of them" (220).

Walker spoke of her abortion to an interviewer in 1973 for the reason so many women have, because "I think it might be important for other women to share" (249). *Meridian* followed in 1976, telling that story again in three forms: the heavily dramatized pain and victimization of Meridian's abortion, the ambiguous sorrow and triumph of Meridian's abandonment of her child, and the reawakened, female-community-based, symbolic maternity of Meridian's compassionate "adoption" of the "child who killed her child," an act like that of Marge Piercy's Jill Stuart whose maternal concern ("Live. Only live.") is for other women who are dying. In 1979 Walker confronted "the child" in an extraordinary speech later published in *In Search of Our Mothers' Gardens* as "One Child of One's Own." No longer "the enemy" to the woman's life or the poet's work, the child in this essay becomes "a meaningful—some might say necessary—digression within the work(s)" of its mother (363). No longer the symbol ("a giant stopper in my throat") of that fear of falling silent, which the poet has discovered is the irreducible "hazard of the work itself" (382) and not of any outside circumstance, the child takes its proper place as "one's friend . . . sister really" (382). Even before this metamorphosis (it didn't happen until her daughter was seven) the infant child, Walker says, "joined me to a body of experience and a depth of commitment to my own life hard to comprehend otherwise" (369).

But the instinct that originally moved Alice Walker to bear a child was less in the mythic sense "maternal" than it was aesthetic and practical. She wanted to save her husband from the draft in 1969 by making him a father. But she was also curious, as an artist and as a woman, about her potential as a parent, about "the child," about the adventure of relationship that would come about after birth.

The necessity of maternal choice is stressed in this essay by Walker's stubborn resistance to the voices of "women's folly" which assailed her *after* Rebecca's birth. These voices insist that once open, the doors of maternity must never close, that the experience of pain, fear, and self-alienation during pregnancy, the possible immobility, conformity, self-divison that motherhood may inflict, have *no reality* beside the miracle of love and the rewards of self-expansion and affirmation.

Perhaps the most illuminating moment in the essay is Walker's account of her own illumination at a viewing of Judy Chicago's *The Dinner Party,* where every dinner plate centers its comment on the guest's womanhood in some working out of a vaginal image— every one but the black woman's plate. Instead, Chicago shows Sojourner Truth as three faces—one weeping, one screaming, one smiling. The unconscious comment, Walker speculates, is that the white world both fears and guiltily affirms the system which decrees that black children are to have less in this world so that white children will have more: "Better then to deny that the black woman has a vagina. Is capable of motherhood. Is a woman" (374).

For Walker, the mother, this moment of insight focuses "the forces of the opposition" on one side of the black woman, forces she must resist with a defense of black maternity, while the forces on the other side, the voices of "women's folly," which call for more and more pregnancies, must simultaneously be resisted. Drawn to and resisting maternity in this way, this one black woman chooses "one child of one's own" but not, in the divinized maternal abstract, "children." Her wary acceptance, her stressful rejection—"*Distance is required, even now*" (369)—is an eloquent echo of the poignant confusion of Claudia MacTeer's "I felt the need for someone to want the black baby to live."

Dream Deferred: *A Raisin in the Sun* and *The Women of Brewster Place*

In Gwendolyn Brooks's 1945 *A Street in Bronzeville* the abortion poem called "the mother" follows "kitchenette building." In this poem the black street dwellers, "greyed in and grey," ponder the possible entrance of the "dream" with its "white and violet . . . aria," then, tired, anxious, mistrusting, turn again to the "lukewarm water" of their lives.[8] "The mother" participates in this same rejection; the dream's searching aria becomes "the voices of my dim killed children," their never-quite-formed breaths now "the voices of the wind," haunting and full of substance, compelling memory in the famous first line of the poem: "Abortions will not let you forget" (5). The "baby ghost" that Linda Bird Francke and so many other women see in their mind's eye, that will become Toni Morrison's avenging/consoling "Beloved," here takes classic shape.

The speaker of the poem entertains briefly the premise that "the crime was not mine," that some defect in her liberation, life in the prison of the "kitchenette building," interfered with her choice: "Believe that even in my deliberation I was not deliberate." She even touches delicately on the satanic side of maternal desire, distancing the metaphor of child-as-candy, as "sweet," to the collective second person: "You will never leave them, controlling your luscious sigh, / Return for a snack of them, with gobbling mother-eye." But the climax of the poem, as Barbara Johnson has noted in "Apostrophe, Animation and Abortion" (32–33), is the discovery that language cannot name the object of the abortion and thus can neither erase nor stabilize the speaker's maternity.

> Since anyhow, you are dead,
> Or rather, or instead,
> You were never made.
> But that too, I am afraid
> Is faulty. (24–28)

Not exactly dead, not exactly made, the speaker's children, emblems of the dream of choice, lie in limbo. The dream is deferred, but not, as Langston Hughes will assert in his 1951 anthem, inert. It does something.

> What happens to a dream deferred?
> Does it dry up
> Like a raisin in the sun?
> Or fester like a sore—
>
> And then run?
> Does it stink like rotten meat?
> Or crust and sugar over—
> Like a syrupy sweet?
>
> Maybe it just sags
> Like a heavy load.
>
> *Or does it explode?*[9]

Two important works with abortion sequences in them by black women writers call for this poem to be printed before their title pages, lending Hughes's abstract images the specificity of pregnancies aborted, corrupted, exploded, undeliverable. Lorraine Hansberry's *A Raisin in the Sun* (1959) and Gloria Naylor's *The Women of Brewster Place* (1982) both depict black women facing maternal choice. In the earlier work black maternity triumphs *as* the dream, and other dreams are deferred. In the later, the enforced abortion is a tragic self-mutilation, but black maternity shows its comic/satanic side, too.

A Raisin in the Sun, central for its exposure of tensions between black American generations and genders, is at one level a hymn to black maternity. Lena Younger, everywhere called Mama, is custodian of the play's preferred female dream of life, growth, birth, while her son Walter Lee's male dream of autonomy, ownership, a share in white capitalism, is deferred, suspect. Three generations of Youngers live in a cramped and sunless Chicago apartment. Like those in Brooks's "kitchenette building," they drive cars and clean house for the white man and woman, barely able to keep Walter's young sister, Beneatha, in clothes for premedical college or Walter's son, Travis, in school lunch money. The family expects a ten-thousand-dollar check from the insurance company after the death of Lena's husband, a hardworking laborer who had been "wild with his women" but loving to his children. A man who "couldn't never catch up with his dreams," but felt that the presence of children validated those dreams.[10]

Everybody has dream plans for the money: Walter wants to buy a share in a liquor store; Beneatha wants to go to medical school; the two mothers, Lena and Walter's wife, Ruth, want to buy a house with sunlight for Mama's plants and room for Ruth's child. The competing dreams build the tension of the first scene, at the end of which Ruth's fainting spell signifies her second pregnancy. Walter's explosive despair—"The future, Mama . . . Just waiting for me—a big, looming blank of space—full of *nothing*" (60)—generates accusations to his women.

> "You wouldn't do nothing to help, would you? You wouldn't be on my side that long for nothing, would you? . . . Man say to his woman: I got me a dream. His woman say: Eat your eggs. Man say: I got to take hold of this here world, baby! And a woman will say: Eat your eggs and go to work." (20, 21)

In despair, Ruth decides to abort the new pregnancy. The first act ends with Mama's challenge to Walter: "Be your father's son. Be the man he was. Your wife say she going to destroy your child. And I'm waiting to hear you talk like him and say we a people who give children life, not who destroys them" (62).

Walter's bitter answer—"we all tied up in a race of people that don't know nothing but moan, pray and have babies" (73)—sets up the gender conflict that carries the rest of the play and illuminates Hansberry's recognition of both the desire for and resistance to black maternity in the community. But Hansberry projects resistance entirely onto the male. Ruth is clearly making Walter's choice, not her own here. Walter's refusal to stop the abortion, his rash handing over of the insurance money (deferring Beneatha's dream) to the con man who promised him partnership in a liquor store, expresses his sense of the choice available to the new black man. He may realize the dream or have the children, not both. Lena's decision to keep one-third of the money as a down payment for a house, and allot Walter only half the money he needs for his dream, signifies her sense of the proper choice: have the child first and chase the dream second, never quite catching up. Mama's assertion that this idea was really her husband's makes the play's apparent shape a struggle between two kinds of manhood signified by two kinds of ownership: the house or the business, the child or the profit. It makes manhood a choice between taking hold of the private self signified by fatherhood but governed by Mama, or taking hold of "this here world."

The plot's every gesture forces Walter towards the female-defined kind of manhood—fatherhood. When he stakes his share and Beneatha's on the liquor store, he loses the money. When, in a last attempt to raise money he insists they sell Lena's newly bought house at the inflated rate the white suburban neighbors will pay them to keep blacks out, he metamorphoses even in his own eyes into the "toothless rat" his sister calls him.

At the same time, whenever Walter makes the "right" moves toward the dream preferred, the play stresses his return to childhood. In a rare, early moment of gentle meditation on the stresses in his marriage, Hansberry's directions comment that *"He is thoughtful, almost as a child would be"* (74). In a moment of loving attention at midplay, before he knows his money has been stolen, he goes to his knees beside Mama and begins singing "All God's Children Got Wings" (102). At the climax, ready, we think, to take the tainted money from the white citizens' association representative, Walter looks into the eyes of his child and changes, becoming, Hansberry's directions say, *"Really like a small boy, looking down at his shoes and then up at the man"* (127). From this ambiguous posture he attains the manhood that is child rooted and childlike, telling "the man" that "we are very proud people. . . . This is my son, who makes the sixth generation of our family in this country, and that we have all thought about your offer and we have decided to move into our house because my father—my father—he earned it" (127–28).

The "man" that grows in Walter at this moment is Mama's child, her "harvest" (124), the "rainbow after the rain" (130).[11] The dreams deferred—Beneatha's medical school, Walter's entrepreneurship—represent the public power and individual ego-gratification which are tainted ideals in the moral universe of the play. Walter stops moaning, eats his eggs, and goes back to work, but the other one-third of his indictment is still correct: Hansberry depicts a strong, proud, and hardworking race that mainly knows how to pray and how to have, and parent, babies. Mama has earlier stopped the free-thinking Beneatha in her tracks— "It's all a matter of ideas, and God is one idea I don't accept" (39)—by reminding her who is really in charge: "Now—you say after me, in my mother's house there is still God" (39). There is a new house at the end of the play, larger, in a better neighborhood. But it is still "my mother's house," and it contains God and, in due time, another child.

Hansberry's play brilliantly exposes the gender tensions exacerbated by racism in her community, resolving them in the enthronement of black maternity. One dream deferred, the heavy load that sags, the child in the womb, is realized. The other, explosive one, represented by Walter and Beneatha, is muted, sugared over. The play's wearily victorious mother expresses no doubts about her way—unless in a curious, final moment, solitary on stage as the lights come down, when *"a great heaving thing rises in her and she puts her fist to her mouth"* (130). When Gloria Naylor comes to write *The Women of Brewster Place,* setting the same Langston Hughes poem at its head, black maternity can no longer carry the whole figurative burden of the dream for the black community, least of all for the women who have invested in it. The novel's "Mama" figure, a strong woman of humor and wisdom named Mattie Michael, long ago left a violent home in order to bear a child whom she speculated might be "the first colored President."[12] But the very density of her love for Basil (a plant that flourishes on the brains of the murdered, as George Eliot's Lydgate morosely reminded us) created "a void in his beauty" (52) that made him irresponsible, narcissistic, finally a deserter. In this novel Mama's manchild ends by depriving her of her house, jumping a bail bond for which the house had been collateral.

It is this male-created houselessness, a condition painfully chronicled in the novel's blues songs ("Then he put me out of doors" [55]) and in Toni Morrison's *The Bluest Eye* as well, that brings Mattie

Michael and the other six women who are the novel's collective protagonist to Brewster Place. This is a run-down, walled-off street which is itself "the bastard child" (1) of white urban political forces never fully understood by any of its residents. Here the women sustain life and each other in the midst of an unbearable tension between sexuality and maternity—a tension magnified, if not created, by the insecurity and violence of the oppressed black male and by the permanently turned back of the white majority.

The story of Mattie's Tennessee friend, the young Lucielia Turner, opens with the funeral of her first baby, who was "the only thing I ever loved without pain" (93). The baby died accidentally, poking a fork into a light socket, but Lucielia blames herself. She had left Serena unsupervised while she had gone yet one more time into the bedroom to try to persuade her lover, the baby's father, to stay with them, to love them, to share her with, and share with her, the maternal being she needs to complement her sexual being. Thus divided, her love "ain't good enough" (100) for the restless and workless Eugene. Lucielia has already made the profoundest, self-alienating sacrifice to keep Eugene. Earlier in the year, finding herself pregnant and listening to his rage and fear—"With two kids and you on my back, I ain't never gonna have nothin' " (95)—she had aborted the second pregnancy. She had lived through "the scraping" and the doctor's "practiced monologue, peppered with sterile kindness" by psychically separating her real self from the woman who chose the abortion (95). But that "other woman" strikes killingly back when the accident happens to the first child, Serena. Full of self-blame, Lucielia attends the funeral and mentally joins what she sees as her two self-murdered children in Serena's coffin, taking to her bed, seeking to die.

In the primitive rebirth scene that follows, Mattie Michael becomes not just the black earth mother but "like a black Brahmin cow, desperate to protect her young," even like "a black mammoth" who "gripped so firmly that the slightest increase of pressure would have cracked [Lucielia's] spine" (103). Her bellowed no to the dying child-mother is "a blasphemous fireball" (102) to the Christian Father God and all the other absent, irresponsible fathers. Her grip on Lucielia, rocking, cradling, ripping her out of death, becomes a huge survey and reversal of the cosmic infanticidal/suicidal impulse projected from fathers and masters onto grieving and maddened mothers.

> Mattie rocked her . . . into a blue vastness just underneath the sun and above time. She rocked her over Aegean seas so clean they shone like crystal, so clear the fresh blood of sacrificed babies torn from their mother's arms and given to Neptune could be seen like pink froth on the water. She rocked her on and on, past Dachau, where soul-gutted Jewish mothers swept their children's entrails off laboratory floors. They flew past the spilled brains of Senegalese infants whose mothers had dashed them on the wooden sides of slave ships. . . . And she rocked her back, back into the womb, to the nadir of her hurt, and they found it,—a slight silver splinter. . . . And Mattie rocked and pulled—and the splinter gave way. (103)

In this scene, recalling Piercy's Jill Stuart and Walker's Meridian with the teenage infanticide, Mattie heals Lucielia by becoming her mother, returning the maddened, infanticidal mother to the life-affirming womb and bearing her again, cleaning the sick and helpless woman "slowly, reverently, as if handling a newborn" (104). In the final moment, newly "virginal" and "baptized" (104), Lucielia drifts toward sleep and a clearer awakening, secured by the mythic maternity of her resilient guardian. As Lena Younger reconceived her son and bore him to manhood in the last scene of *Raisin*, so does Mattie reverse the self-hating womanhood of her adopted daughter, rebearing her in the final scene of her story.

The next story in *The Women of Brewster Place* however, one obliquely shaded with allusions to *A Midsummer Night's Dream*, seems to defer the morning's awakening, picturing not a mythic but a satanically obsessive maternity, a black-comic enthronement of the eternal baby. It tells of Cora Lee, who as a child, even a teenager, refused all gifts, toys, and occupations except the "ritual" of the baby doll. As the daughter's body began to ripen the father shuddered at her obsessive suckling of "the dead brown plastic" (108), and her mother finally explained to her that the games the neighbor boy was teaching Cora Lee about "the thing that felt good in the dark" were forbidden, because "her body could now make babies"

(109). The "disjointed mysteries of life," sexuality and maternity, were thus rejoined ominously and simplistically for Cora Lee, and the story jumps to a comically nightmarish scene five (or is it eight?) babies later. Children of all ages swarm in her crowded welfare flat on dead-end Brewster Place, hopelessly out of control, while the child who desired motherhood to avoid womanhood broods on the unaccountable process by which what she loves, the brand new baby "who could be fed from her body" (112), becomes the crowd of children, persons, whose needs cannot be met from her body or her inert fantasy maternity.

Babies "stayed where you put them" (112), allowing Cora Lee to plug into the soap operas which replay her own maternity obsessions: "Steve's murder trial. . . . Jessica's secret abortion. . . . If Rachel had divorced Mack because he's become impotent after getting caught in that earthquake" (110–18). Children expose her to the world of welfare workers and food stamps, nagging teachers, and helpful or critical neighbors who break up the fantasy/security, the narcissism, of the mother-baby dyad. One or two fathers dimly attached to "the thing that felt good in the dark" have made a brief impression on Cora, but they declared themselves incompatible with babies crying and so left. Now she feels comfortable with the male "shadows" who come and go, supplying the babies, enforcing no intimacy.

A brief awakening from this dream of maternity, crusted and sugared over like a syrupy sweet, occurs ironically when a young rent strike organizer talks Cora Lee into taking her ragged, quarreling, intelligent, and neglected children to an all-black performance of *A Midsummer Night's Dream*. She uses soap operas to validate a maternal obsession fixed and arrested at age seven, but her own children need art to show them, and her, their adult possibilities. Watching Titania, Cora Lee intuits her daughter's potential queenship. Once Maybelline had liked school, once Sammy had written rhymes on the bathroom walls. But their mother's unresponsiveness or criticism had deflected and distorted their ambitions until Maybelline began to tear up library books instead of reading them, and Sammy now seeks the sweets his mother psychically denies him by eating out of garbage cans. Cora wanted her babies to grow up directly into insurance salesmen and doctors and lawyers; when they become children and teenagers instead, she calls them "dumb asses." Brucie, watching Bottom, asks anxiously if that face is his future, and Cora Lee stirs out of her dream, recognizing her guilt, determining to take up her responsibility.

But the story's ending is ambiguous. Her children asleep, Cora Lee returns to her own bed, accepts another anonymous male shadow into it, "turned and folded her evening like gold and lavender gauze, deep within the creases of her dreams" (127). Like the "grotesque" figures in Sherwood Anderson's *Winesburg, Ohio,* which *The Women of Brewster Place* often resembles in style and theme, Cora Lee has been captured by a truth (someone does want black babies to live) too fierce to admit of other complexifying truths.[13]

Conversations with the Dead: *The Bluest Eye* and *Beloved*

Toni Morrison's *The Bluest Eye* (1970) charts black maternity on a trajectory from need through love, incest, and rape, to pregnancy, fetal death, and maternal madness. At the novel's apex, a dialogue occurs between the child-mother and an italicized voice who speaks from behind Pecola's eyes, from under her heart, from her side—a motherly, sisterly, daughterly voice at once consoling and probing, a voice I take to be, at the deepest level, the voice of her dead fetus.

So viewed, this compelling and difficult scene offers a link not only between Morrison's first novel and her most recent one, *Beloved* (1987), but also between the abortion topos as offered by Gwendolyn Brooks ("You remember the children you got that you did not get") and a more radical project current in much black female writing. This project is the depiction of a domain of spirit in which the ancestral dead and the dream deferred, the dim killed children and the enslaved, often killing mothers, speak in probing healing, summoned by the living in an act of agonized remembering which aims to embody, make whole, a community, a race, not only an individual psyche.

The project is evident in the brilliant technical creation of such a domain in Gayle Jones's *Corregidora* or Toni Cade Bambara's *The Salt*

Eaters. It is validated in Alice Walker's insouciant and serious after-note to *The Color Purple:* "I thank everybody in this book for coming. A. W. author and medium." Toni Morrison refers to it in a recent reply about *Beloved* to interviewer Marsha Darling: "When you say 'channeling,' I'm taking that to mean part of what writing is for me, which is to have an idea and to know that it's alive, that things may happen to it if I am available to a character or a presence or some information that does not come out of any research that I've done."[14]

So. Called up not (alone) by "research," not (alone) as metaphor for, or projection of, a contemporary distress, a "presence" speaks eerily from and with these texts, communicating simultaneously from the mutilated past and the inchoate, compromised future: the child, the parent, that you got but you did not get. Let us look at the "presence" in a first appearance, in *The Bluest Eye.*

Black infanticide is at the heart of the novel's plot. In 1940, in Lorain, Ohio, the southern cultural archetype that diverted black maternity toward the care and worship of the white infant has moved north without its accompanying condition. The bereft black baby, once marketable, may no longer be sold, must simply be erased. The novel's three black female protagonists, Frieda and Claudia MacTeer, aged ten and nine, and Pecola Breedlove, aged twelve, are already part of this process: they sicken with possessive love of the white infant icons—golden baby dolls, perky Shirley Temple, the blue-eyed Mary Jane on the candy bar—which they are offered at every turn. Strong with the tainted strength of an orderly, middle-class black upbringing, the narrating Claudia recalls that she once dismembered white dolls (22) and, in her imagination, white children, half in rage, half in confused search for the beauty which was denied her, before she learned that guilty "adjustment" from rage to shame to love of the white object and hatred of the black, which her society demanded, which was "adjustment without improvement" (22). Tenacious with the doomed endurance of a child isolated in a chaotically self-hating, poor black family, the scapegoated Pecola practiced "disappearing" herself (only the black eyes wouldn't "go") until the arrival of puberty opened a new and dangerous vista.

"Is it true that I can have a baby now?"

"Sure," said Frieda drowsily. "Sure you can."

"But . . . how?" Her voice was hollow with wonder.

"Oh," said Frieda, "somebody has to love you." . . .

Then Pecola asked a question that had never entered her mind. "How do you do that? I mean, how do you get somebody to love you?" (29)

As the novel's grim "Autumn" moves into its "Winter" section, Pecola ponders the revelation that her whore friend, Miss Marie, did once love a man and bear children, while "into her eyes came the picture of Cholly and Mrs. Breedlove in bed" (48). The two scenes lock together, one producing "choking sounds and silence" (49), the other that baby, baby doll, who would love her, *be* her. The special "agitation" that overcomes Pecola during a scene when her male schoolmates pelt her with a contemptuous rhyme, "Black e mo Black e mo Ya daddy sleeps nekkid" (55, 59), is the mark of her innocent and tragic prayer for a triple "miracle" whose parts only *seem* contradictory: to disappear, to have blue eyes, to have the love that produces a baby.

"Winter" climaxes with a little death for Pecola. Invited by a spiteful playmate into his immaculate, middle-class brown home, the "Black e mo" girl is attracted by the "blue ice" eyes of a "deep silky black" cat (74), the image of her desired self. Jealous of her rapport with it, the young boy snatches the cat away, swings it around his head, and accidentally smashes it against a wall. The boy's mother returns. Rejecting Pecola's needy eyes and black skin as she has rejected "the funk of her own being" (68), she screams at the little girl in rage. The limp cat, which seemed to be dead, revives, taking Pecola's proper place in the maternal bosom. The scene exactly anticipates the terrible "Spring" scene in which Pecola's mother, Pauline, chooses the "pink and yellow child" (87) of her employers after Pecola upsets a blackberry pie in the clean, white kitchen which Pauline has internalized, along with everything white, as her own. Pauline's hissed words to her daughter—"Crazy fool . . . crazy"—are not only a rejection, but a direction also.

This maternal rejection confirms Pecola's maternal desire to have a mother/be a mother, a desire coterminous with self-erasure. It is this complex amalgam, as well as the wild mixture of tenderness, hatred, and anomie in the emotionally "disfunctional" (126) black father, that makes the rape scene which follows it so disturbing. Motherless, fatherless, loveless, planless, Cholly Breedlove is by this time a mere atom of half-consciousness. He owns no bond, seeks no connection between one moment and the next, between desire and act; he is "dangerously free" (125). He is poles apart from the powerful Victorian patriarch of *Waterland*, whose incestuous love is another, ultimately self-destructive form of his society's approved entrepreneurialism; poles apart even from the self-possessed black father of *The Cider House Rules*, whose incest is another index of his control of his own life. Deeply unaccommodated, Cholly has no myth of control at all, only an occasional "floodlit break," while he drinks, between one oblivion and the next (126).

The narrative audaciously and disturbingly takes his perspective, if not his part, as he forces his silent daughter: "He was conscious of her wet soapy hands on his wrists, the fingers clenching, but whether her grip was from a hopeless but stubborn struggle to be free, or from some other emotion, he could not tell" (128).[15] Only the reader, privileged by the confidences and the images of the novel's narrator, can tell what some of these other emotions might have been—maternal desire, self-erasure, love.

The novel's time frame begins in straight realism: "There were no marigolds in the fall of 1941. We thought, at the time, that it was because Pecola was having her father's baby that the marigolds did not grow" (9). Its formal shape—sections titled "Autumn," "Winter," "Spring," "Summer"—seems at first in a time line with this, a simple structure of flashback. Yet the stable, past tense speech of both the omniscient narrator and the engaged narrator, Claudia MacTeer, consistently begins in, and continually returns to, a mystified, present tense, mythic space which is not simply a deeply animated memory, but a real domain of presence. Here, in timeless repetition, black things are destroyed, women lean out of windows, men touch the forbidden and anguishing bodies of girl-children.[16] Here, eternally, Pecola "looks up . . . and sees the vacuum where curiosity ought to lodge. And something more, the total absence of human recognition—the glazed separateness" (42). Here Claudia shoulders the guilt of her early denial even as she expiates it in the recognition of her narrative: "When the land kills of its own volition, we acquiesce and say the victim had no right to live. We are wrong, of course, but it doesn't matter. It's too late" (160). And here the framing text of a white suburban Dick and Jane reader hovers forever between freezing irony and dynamic presence: "LOOKLOOKHERECOMESAFRIENDTHEFRIENDWILLPLAYWITH JANETHEYWILLPLAYAGOODGAMEPLAYJANEPLAY" (152).

"The friend" who comes to play with Pecola in this climactic chapter is many things. She is the intimate Claudia and the maternal Pauline who never came, or came too late, to her; the Shirley Temple, the Mary Jane, the Maureen Peel, the black cat with blue eyes who stole the world's love and might at last share. She is the Mr. Henry, Cholly Breedlove, Soaphead Church, or even God, whose game of manipulation masks an impotent love and who might perform the miracle of unjudging guidance.

"The friend" comes in some timeless time just after the hot summer afternoon when the charlatan, Soaphead Church, appealed to by the pregnant Pecola for the miracle of blue eyes, affects to grant her this boon in exchange for the little girl's unknowing participation in the killing of an old dog nearby who is annoying him. She comes in the narrative just before the fall day when the reader learns that the baby "came too soon and died" (158) like (perhaps *when*) the dog died. She comes before Claudia tells us that Pecola "stepped over into madness" (159).

The friend's presence is healing, probing, therapeutic. Her italicized dialogue makes her seem sometimes a spirited contemporary: "[Maureen] sure is popular." *"Who wants to be popular?"* "Not Me." *"Me neither"* (152). Sometimes a consoling mother: "I was so lonely. . . . And you were right here. Right before my eyes" *"No, honey. Right after your eyes"* (152). The friend, unshakably black-eyed herself, alternately challenges Pecola's fixation on what she believes is her new set of blue eyes: *"I'd just like to do something besides watch you stare in that mirror"* (150). Assuages it: "Are they really nice?" *"Yes, very nice."* "Just 'very nice'?" *"Really, truly, very nice"* (151). Challenges again: "Really, truely bluely nice?" *"Oh,*

God. You are crazy." "I am not!" "I didn't mean it that way" (151). The friend is the black-eyed self, black-eyed baby doll, black-eyed baby, whom the newly, truly bluely eyed Pecola has left behind, killed like the dog in response to the furies of her internalized white compulsions.

The friend, it appears, has two main tasks: to save Pecola and to bring her to face the barely nameable complex of emotions that animate her compulsions; to turn her away from the godlike mirror of her blue eyes (*"Look, I can look right at the sun." "Don't do that!"* [151]) to face her black eyes. And the key figure in that mirror is her father.

> *She* [Pauline] *probably misses him.*
> I don't know why she would. All he did was get drunk and beat her up. . . .
> *Well, she probably loved him anyway.*
> Him?
> *Sure, why not, Anyway, if she didn't love him, she sure let him do it to her a lot. . . .*
> She didn't like it.
> *Then why did she let him do it to her?*
> Because he made her.
> *How could somebody make you do something like that?*
> Easy.
> *Oh yeah, How easy?*
> They just make you, that's all.
> *I guess you're right. And Cholly could make anybody do anything.*
> He could not.
> *He made you, didn't he?*
> Shut up!

Gently pursuing, backing off when necessary, the friend elicits the information that Cholly sexually approached his daughter a second time, while she was reading on the sofa, that "hated piece of furniture" which "imposed a furtiveness on the loving done on it," that new piece which arrived already "split," pervading the room and its life with "joylessness" (32). "The first time" with Cholly, described for us, was certainly horrible, but the second time (*"The second time too?" "Yes." "Really?"*) is still buried in denial ("Leave me alone! You better leave me alone!" [156]).

It seems likely that "the second time" of incestuous rape included, simultaneous with its horror, some mixture of the desire/ compulsion for death as black, rebirth as white and in possession of the love/lover (self, paternal, maternal) most clearly crystallized in the figure of the loving, needing infant. If so, then this scene of analysis, therapist "presence" to victim, doesn't "work," cannot make that seed of knowledge in Pecola blossom into self-acceptance and sanity, or into a loved black self or black baby, any more than the earth can produce Claudia's marigold. Perhaps the narrative, committed to its tragic myth, or even the novelist, hesitating before the demonism of black maternal desire which gives *away* the beloved self to the figure of the child, cannot sufficiently want this black baby to live.

But the dialogue here is not only a scene of analysis. It is also a magic scene, a child's version of the "conjuring and root working" that marked African-American forms of appeal to the domain of spirit. In the paragraph before it, Claudia and Frieda plant the seeds that testify to their desire to have "somebody" want the black baby to live. The two girls agree to "make the miracle" and enter into a dialogue of word and song: "Let me [Claudia] sing this time." "You [Frieda] say the magic words" (149). On this level, as the dialogue continues, Claudia singing Pecola's obsessive lament and the more matter-of-fact Frieda speaking "the friend's" words of self-discovery and growth, the magic seems to work for a time, then it fails. Narrating Claudia's Pecola self can't break out of its obsession, and Frieda's survivalist MacTeer self, black survivalist sanity to Pecola's lyric compulsions, finally deserts her, exasperated, and perhaps frightened.

> *I'm not going to play with you anymore.*
> Oh, Don't leave me.
> *Yes, I am.*
> Why, Are you mad at me?
> *Yes.*

Because my eyes aren't blue enough? . . .
No. Because you're acting silly. (158)

Because they failed her, because, cruelly self-protective in their own self-accusation, her madness "bored us in the end" (159), because in her madness, Pecola acted silly forever, the MacTeers "avoided Pecola Breedlove—forever" (158).

Yet there is a third possibility, another mystery, invoked by this dialogue. Therapist, playmate, the unnamed italicized "presence" seems to hold all the cards, have all the answers. One time only, however, Pecola seems to drive the "presence" into an evasion of her own.

Where do you live?
I told you once.
What is your mother's name?
Why are you so busy meddling me?

Briefly materializing here as daughter-presence, the friend all but names Pecola her mother, suddenly lighting up the deeply hidden corners of this apparently father-centered dialogue which has in fact been about maternal daughterhood: "Ever since I got my blue eyes, she look away from me all the time. Do you suppose she's jealous?" (151), *"Maybe she doesn't feel too good since Cholly's gone"* (155), and *"Why didn't you tell Mrs. Breedlove?"* "She wouldn't have believed me" (155). Traumatized by her mother's neglect, her portentous absence, Pecola reaches out in this dialogue for her mother through her daughter. In the end, she cannot overcome that absence. Instead, tragically, increasingly, she imitates it: "Shut up! Shut up!" (154), "Leave me alone" (155), "Leave me alone" (156). Ultimately, she precipitates the absence she fears: "Please help me look." *"No"* (157); "Don't leave me." *"Yes, I am"* (158).

In the last moment of the dialogue, the friend promises to return. Where she went, or who she came from—was it from the narrative of Claudia, who despairs, or of the omniscient framing narrator, who embracingly reports?—or whether she will return, is ambiguous. Pecola "stepped over into madness" (159), Claudia says, but whether to join the recovered, forgiving daughter-presence, or in grief at its absence, we do not know. Morrison's latest novel, *Beloved*, set in an earlier time, offers no certain answers either, but it does expand, in time, space, and spirit, the question.

*

C onversations with the aborted future end either in silence or in miracle. And even when the resurrection happens, when, for instance, *The Salt Eaters*'s suicidal Velma Henry takes flight, dropping her shawl like the pieces of a "burst cocoon," or the whole colored community of that novel seems in miraculous simplicity to wheel sharply away from its flight towards violence and death like a flock of birds intuitively changing direction, the narrative must hint at the future squandering or forgetting of that moment.[17] But conversations with the past are in their nature sustained resurrections of the figures of the past, of the summoner in the present, and of the idea of a future. For the present is the past's future. In a powerful series of novels summoning the slave ancestors for conversation, black women writers make present not only the generations that have issue, the stories that have been "passed," but also, in a supreme act of imaginative remembering, the generations that did not have issue: the mothers who killed, the children who died, rather than engage with the infamy of slavery, and the stories that were not passed, because they would wither, rather than inspirit, the heart of the hearer.

Sherley A. Williams's 1986 *Dessa Rose*, set in pre–Civil War Carolina and points west, depicts the black maternal investment as coterminous with freedom *and* future, but it is keenly aware of its bitter ambiguity. The slave Odessa, beaten, pregnant, escapes twice with the help of fellow slaves to come to brief rest and give birth at the farm of a sympathetic white woman, Ruth. Eventually, the white woman and her "slaves" all form an ingenious plan to escape from the white-male-ruled claustrophobia of the South. The white woman travels from town to town, east to west, "selling" the black men and women over and over as they escape and return: the shared money thus made provides for the eventual movement of the white woman to the Northeast and the free black community to the West. (This same movement, interestingly, takes the sympathetic, white "cracker" woman, Amy, who helps Toni Morrison's

Sethe in *Beloved*, to Boston, while Sethe and the other blacks go northwest across the Ohio to Cincinnati.)

Even among this escaping community, however, the whips of sexism cut still deeper than those of racism. The blacks learn finally to trust the whiteness of Ruth, but womanhood, especially black womanhood, is never given its full human due. Despite himself the black man Ned calls Dessa "an old mule," and Dessa trembles to see white male contempt "loosed against one of us" from someone black who was "part of us."[18] She bitterly counts the burdened women of her memory: Molly, who had seventeen children and was then sold when she ceased bearing; Flora, who "broke" under the selling of her children; Janet, beaten because she was barren; Ada, whose white master desired her and their daughter both; and Dessa herself, whose death sentence after her first escape was postponed until she could deliver a marketable baby (198–99).

In the novel's opening section, the unspeakably vile and voy-euristic white writer, Nehemiah, recording interesting and salacious tidbits about "the darky" for a white southern readership, learns to his shock that Dessa chose to continue her pregnancy. She refused the often welcome services of the black community's abortionist de-spite her recognition of the likely fate of a black woman's child under slavery, because the father of the child was someone she loved (43). Dessa persuaded the embittered lover to agree, despite his fears for the future, for "it was her heart, *his* heart, that Kaine asked her to kill" (43). Ultimately that heart becomes a mouth for passing on the story: "Well, *this* the childrens have heard from our own lips. I hope they never have to pay what it cost us to own our-selfs. . . . Oh, we have paid for our children's place in the world again, and again. . . " (260). We have seen the image of the fetus within as the heart of the mother before, in the words of the teenage infanticide whom Alice Walker's *Meridian* meets at the end of the novel; we will see Toni Morrison use it again in *Beloved*, as the red heart becomes the innermost part of the self, turned inside out to speak its urgent need.

Gayle Jones's 1970 *Corregidora* depicts a line of black women in-cestuously fathered by a Portuguese slave owner-breeder. The women—Ursa Corregidora's mother, grandmother, great-grandmother—steadfastly and subversively have children, "make generations" (10) in order to pass on the story, "hold up the evidence" (14) of what "they," white men, did to "us," black women. But there is one story not told, only hinted at. There was something Great Gran, the original African, the "coffee-bean woman," degraded and enslaved but mysteriously a figure of power also, did to old Corregidora, something that showed the slaver his own vulnerability, his own death, something that eventually drove him crazy. Ursa, fighting her lover, Mutt, for an independent space of being, for the blues-singing jobs she knows will bring that space, is knocked down the stairs by him, losing their recently conceived fetus and her womb as well in the subsequent miscarriage. She cannot now make generations and so relieve herself of the agony of her foremothers' stories of male victimization, the "suppressed hysteria" (59) transmitted to, but also by, daughters. And even if she could have the desired daughter, she asks herself, "Would I have kept it up? Would I have been like *her*, or *them*?" (60), like the original ancestress, who somehow "did something" that enabled her to keep on feeling, or the daughters, mulatto women, who felt nothing for any man but the hysteria that demands daughters to pass on the story.

For the daughters, Corregidora's women, all men are Corregidora, the demon spoilers. Fighting her lover, Ursa is fighting and perpetuating Corregidora. Only in the novel's final pages, after twenty-two years of independence and solitude, does Ursa give herself to Mutt again, offering him what he wants most and never got from her before, an act of oral sex portrayed as actively gentle, maternal, as if she were sucking poison from the wound of a child. In the split-second before her teeth close on the vulnerable organ, Ursa understands, receives in wordless conversation with the dead coffee-bean woman, what Great Gran "did" to Corregidora. Castration, whether in the act or in the shadow, the conception of the act, makes man vulnerable to woman, equal. And though it is a negative equality that Ursa and Mutt, and perhaps momentarily Corregidora and Great Gran, discover in that split second—" 'I don't want a kind of woman that hurt you,' he said. . . . 'I don't want a kind of man that'll hurt me neither,' I said"—it makes a foundation—"He held me tight" (185). The relationship that Mutt and Ursa achieve suffers no lack in the absence of a child. The victory Ursa wins is the consolidation of a self that knows its being and value through multiple feelings, not alone through the investment of all that is precious, all that is evidence, "presence," in a child. This is the climactic illumination in Morrison's *Beloved*, too. Here the urgent mission of black maternity, arising out of the experience of genocide in the days of slavery, has curved past the obsessive generation making of Corregidora's women and become the thing it fled. Rather than return herself, her two daughters, and her two sons to the man who has just caught them, the escaped slave Sethe had made to kill all her four children and succeeded in killing one daughter. After eight years of a life lived in thrall to that haunting presence, Sethe is joined by Paul D, a fellow slave, fellow sufferer. His role is ultimately to exorcise the beloved, enraged, engorging child "presence." Bereft at the end, Sethe cries, "She was my best thing," and Paul counters, with what feels like the authority of the narrative itself, "You your best thing, Sethe. You are."[19]

Not one but two unspeakable acts stare at one another through the years and pages of *Beloved*, forming a yin-yang figure which illuminates as well as anything in literature the Armageddon of the maternal instinct. This figure yields a spectrum of signs to readers inside and outside the novel: it signifies brute, animal maternity, gutted, gutting, the sow eating its farrow, as well as mythic, mystic maternity, from the sanctifying milk of the virgin mother to the ecstatic tears of the pietà. In between, beleaguered, lies human maternity.

Julia Kristeva defines human maternity as "the ambivalent principle that is bound to the species on the one hand, and on the other stems from an identity catastrophe that causes the Name to topple over into the unnameable that one imagines as femininity, non-language, or body."[20] This identity "catastrophe," the continual "toppling" from the stable name of the "I" to the constellations of process and matter (and psycho-moral impulse) imposed by the biological and social constructs of maternity, is especially powerful in the case of *Beloved*'s black maternal protagonist. Her "white" name is Jenny, conferred by owners; her black name, her father's name, Sethe, conferred on her in whispers by her absent mother's friend out of an African language now erased from her memory. At the penultimate moment of extremity, a slave crawling half-dead to the river beyond which her escaped children wait, Sethe exists only *as* that ambivalent maternal principle, not in touch with her own life, only "concerned for the life of the mother of her children" (30). At the ultimate extremity, when Sethe faces the slavecatcher, that alienated and ambivalent principle can express its concern for life, its bond to the species, only in slaughter.

It is a horrific pietà that black neighbors and white slavecatchers see in the coldshed at 124 Bluestone Road, Cincinnati, in the summer of 1855: "Inside two boys bled in the sawdust and dirt at the feet of a nigger woman holding a bloodsoaked child to her chest with one hand and an infant by the heels in the other" (149). The slavecatchers depart, minus their now worthless prey; the abolitionist societies make sentimental capital of a slave mother's tragic madness and manage to save Sethe from hanging. The black community could understand one part of her motivation: "Collected every bit of life she had made, all the parts of her that were precious and fine and beautiful, and carried, pushed, dragged them through the veil, out, away, over there where no one could hurt them. Over there" (163). They scent and disapprove of the pride in the godlike possessiveness of "life she had made," but miss the deep self-alienation of "parts of her that were precious." Appalled, they withdraw from the blindly self-sufficient woman who comes out of jail to continue living "her unliveable life" (113).

But another more crucially personal scene of horror lies behind the almost wordless cry, "No. No. Nono. Nonono" (163), that drives Sethe to the shed and the rusty sawblade and the killing of her first daughter, a complex and shattering scene of maternal degradation that took place at Sweet Home Farm the day Sethe and her husband, Halle, were scheduled to escape with their children and others across the river from Kentucky. Sethe's account to fellow slave Paul D begins matter of factly as he asks what caused the mass of scars in the shape of a tree on her back: "These boys come in there and took my milk. That's what they came in there for. Held me down and took it. . . . Them boys found out I told on 'em. School-teacher made one open up my back, and when it closed it made a tree" (17). Listening, Paul D's quiet inquiries, and Sethe's monotone replies, make it clear that, manlike, however empathetic, Paul D has missed the point.

> "They used cowhide on you?"
> "And they took my milk."
> "They beat you and you was pregnant?"
> "And they took my milk." (17)

Perhaps he is deliberately evading the point, one that can "break" a man if he sees it too clearly. Later Paul D gives Sethe the painful news that Halle, her husband, must have witnessed that dreadful milking, because "something broke him" that day, and he ended up speech-less, mad, "rubbing butter all over his face by the churn" (68–69).

No one but Sethe and, disturbingly, the reader, ever knows the last, most terrible, fragment of that scene, however: "Two boys with mossy teeth, one sucking on my breast, the other holding me down, their book-reading teacher watching and writing it up" (70).

Writing it up. Nothing makes the skin crawl, rouses the human horror of identity being sunk below even the animal into the object, like this detail. Bad enough to be a black mother whose nursing milk goes first to white babies, then, maybe, to your own. Bad enough to send your child ahead to freedom while you remain be-hind carrying the milk she needs. Terrible to have it stolen once again in an act of bestial rape, demonic nursing, by another white: "They handled me like I was the cow, no, the goat" (200). Tragic to find that the black husband, who witnessed this ultimate act con-firming the white view of the animality of the black that he has struggled all his life not to believe, was destroyed by it. But to have the white man who had for the past six months been writing a book on "the human and animal characteristics" of his black slaves (193) enforce that degradation, in a moment of casual experimentation, by setting his nephew to milk that animal and then "write it up" with ink she herself had made—this is to make the citadel of black maternity, virtually of black identity, fairly rock. This indeed is "writing with the body"—a coerced patriarchal triumph. White milk from black breasts becomes black ink on the white pages of a vast and inescapable falsehood. Black maternity is removed from the realm of the human, and insofar as black female, and even Halle's black male, identity is dependent on black maternity, identity falls.

This is the world, white erasing black, white male erasing female, animal erasing human, which Sethe rejects for her children and herself when she sees the schoolteacher's hat the day the slave-catcher finds her and her children. Halle's friend Paul D, now Sethe's lover, has lived in this same world, suffered a similar erasure, bitted like a horse at Sweet Home Farm, driven like a mule on the chain gangs of Georgia. He should, like the implied reader of *Beloved*, stand abashed and incapable of judgment when the revelation of Sethe's infanticidal "rescue" comes to join the revelation of her dreadful milking. Yet he does judge, and in terms that re-open the deepest of her wounds and deny the mutuality of the erasure black woman and black man have suffered.

> "What you did was wrong, Sethe."
> "I should have gone back there? Taken my babies back there?"
> "There could have been a way. Some other way."
> "What way?"
> "You got two feet, Sethe, not four," he said, and right then a forest sprang up between them, trackless and wild.
> (165)

This desertion is the climax of the novel's first book. But Paul D's judgment was not entirely his own at that moment. Something of its harshness, its unerring, rhetorically wounding point, was contributed by the "presence" observing the scene "through the ceiling" (165), by the mysteriously knowing and unknown young woman who walked out of the river and into the household just as Sethe, Paul D, and Denver, her remaining daughter, were beginning to forget the past and form a family. She claims the name "Beloved," the name Sethe had put on the tombstone of her self-murdered daughter. And she is the stuff of nightmare as well as of dream. Like the "friend" who comes to play with Pecola in *The Bluest Eye,* Beloved is many persons. Unlike her she is a real person, but she is also created out of the separate, hidden, psychic agendas of the three inhabitants of 124 Bluestone Road, the emblem of the hidden rage and desire of three people who have "successfully" adapted to the "unliveable life" of the African-American.

For Sethe, increasingly, she is the embodied ghost of the daughter whose killing she is beyond "justifying" but whose absence is intolerable. For Denver, she is the sister who can assuage the loneliness of a life lived with an ambiguously loved/feared murderess-mother in a house the community shuns. A spooky, invisible "presence" in the years since the killing, "the baby" made the house glow and smoke with her spite and jealousy, broke crockery and the limbs of any dweller unfortunate enough to resist her, or resist Denver's and Sethe's separate preoccupations with her.

When Paul D walks into the house, eighteen years after the baby's death, the "presence" drowns him in "a pool of pulsing red light" (9), pitches him against the walls, pelts him with abuse. He fights it, "screaming back at the screaming house" (18), and seems to drive it away. But when Beloved, beautiful, nineteen (like Sethe and Paul D were at Sweet Home; like the baby would be now), comes into 124 Bluestone, she comes summoned by a secret rage in him, too. Sethe had felt the heart of the baby she had killed continue beating in her hand after it had died (198). And Paul D believes that he has killed his own heart in order to survive the inevitable death of everything he has loved or could be tempted to love: "He would keep [the memories] in that tobacco tin buried in his chest where a red heart used to be. Its lid rusted shut" (72–73). But man, like woman, hungers for that red heart of the self. When, in malice, the girl Beloved seduces him, Paul, in anguish, receives back the heart. Her "inside part" ("You have to touch me. On the inside part.") is also his: "What he knew was that when he reached the inside part he was saying, 'Red heart. Red heart' over and over again" (117).

A psychologist would note, as Paul D himself does, that the woods and rivers of postwar Ohio were full of young black women like the one who came to their house, women "drifting from ruin" (152).

Locked out of their own identity by unspeakable sorrow or humiliation, they can become a habitation for the ghosts of others: the psychokinetic energy of the murdering mother and the almost murdered daughter, which made a living person of the house at 124 Bluestone Road, now makes a dwelling in the emptied eyes of the stranger. She acquires through that energy the slaughter marks of the ghost sister-daughter; she does the deeds that figure would do. Her choking fingers around Sethe's neck are the baby's, and Denver's, and Sethe's own. Her relaxation of the murdering circle, leaving bruises but no broken bones, is Sethe's, and Denver's, and the baby's forgiveness (96–97). Her seduction of Paul is Denver's own desire to "move" him out of the original triad—mother, living daughter, "baby ghost." Above all, the "longing" in her actually expressionless eyes is Sethe's murdered daughter's longing, enraged and loving, for her mother. As the world narrows down to that one room which is the empty mind of Beloved (183), receiving/ radiating the hunger of the two women present and that of the absent man, a new roaring is heard by those who pass by 124 Bluestone Road, "a conflagration of hasty voices" of which only one word can be deciphered—"mine" (172).

A psychologist would say that the novel follows black identity on a trajectory from silence, the virtual erasure of identity by white patriarchy, to this roaring "mine," an identity desperately pursued first by projecting being outside the self, preeminently onto a child, and then desperately, pitilessly gripping that outside projection as "me," an identity, a red heart that is inside a self-loved body. "Motherlove is a killer" (132), when the child who is "mine" is also "me." So is daughterlove, as the novel graphically demonstrates when, subsumed in the dyad she could not free herself from, Sethe becomes thinned down and dried up in the wind of Beloved's love, ultimately vomiting the food not she but Beloved has eaten (243).

A psychologist would say all these things, but Morrison's narrative believes in the spirit world as well as in the psychological one, keeping a delicate balance between the catastrophes that the structure of narrative requires be humanly resolved, those that require the cooperation of "the ancestors" to come within structure, and those that no narrative can close, no story "pass on," or pass by.

The eighteen-year old Denver learns her "me" when she leaves the roaring house to find food, work, in order to protect the dyad which is "mine," which she identifies with, from killing itself. A young friend's casual "Take care of yourself, Denver" teaches her a deep truth, however; that her instinctive feeling that "Somebody had to be saved" referred not only to Beloved and Sethe, but to Denver herself: "It was a new thought, having a self to look out for and preserve" (252).

Sethe discovers her "me" at the hands of Paul D in a scene at the end of the novel which revives and reverses the original killing scene, what the "holy" matriarch, Baby Suggs, Sethe's mother-in-law, had called The Misery. After Denver had made the break from the house, the community had responded with food and help, even the Quaker white man, Edward Bodnar, who rode out to 124 Bluestone Road to bring back Denver to give her permanent work. The white rider, hatted like her old enemy schoolteacher, triggers the old desperation, and Sethe goes after him with an ice pick. Denver, wrestling her down, saves the man, and her mother, from death. Paul D, drawn by some mysterious force to return, finds Sethe lying in bed, exhausted, but ready for change.

Her first words, "I made the ink, Paul D. He couldn't have done it if I hadn't made the ink" (277), suggest that she lives no more in a simple world of malign forces where the only possible response is "No. No. Nono. Nonono," but rather is ready to shoulder the responsibility of her "I." She also shoulders, in this complex, rhetorical figure, her share of the burden of literacy enabling and haunting the civilization of the West. Sethe is in parts of the novel an oral narrator of her story, achieving in that way the self-discovery central to the autobiographical process that, as Valerie Smith argues, structures so much black American fiction.[21] By the end, her recognition of her own complicity, ink maker, in the white *writing*-out of her authentic humanity, signals, I think, her readiness to take the ink for herself. It makes her somehow a narrating partner, speaking/writing with the novelist.

In a move which reflects the early caretaking of women for women in the novel, that also reminds the reader of the bathing/birthing episode between Mattie Michael and Lucielia in *The Women of*

Brewster Place, Paul D prepares at the end of the novel to bathe Sethe. Imagining his touch, part by part, restoring and gathering a body of whose existence she has never been sure since the multiple erasure and "topplings" of slavery and maternity and desertion, Sethe sees a new citadel of identity. She holds on briefly to the old citadel: now that the mysterious Beloved has disappeared in the aftermath of the ice pick incident, Sethe mourns again, in the loss of her "child," the loss of her "best thing." But Paul D draws her away from that, saying, "You your best thing," and Sethe's wondering response, "Me? Me?" has the quality not of doubt but of discovery (273).

And Beloved herself? A palpably living being, pregnant with Paul D's child, naked, beautiful, disappearing into the woods at novel's end, she is all the voices of Gwendolyn Brooks's "dim killed children." She is the story that cannot be passed on (275), the roaring "mine" that cannot be assembled into a "me." Even after the barely speakable story of the black male, iron collared and steel bitted, lies down next to the story of the black female, milked and murdering, after Paul D "put his story next to Sethe's" (273) and together they assuage "the loneliness that can be rocked" (274), there is still another "loneliness that roams" (274), untouchable, unassuageable. Beloved is the daughter that Sethe killed in half-holy horror. She is also a sister: she is the enforced pregnancy after rape by white crew members whose "product" Sethe's mother threw overboard at birth, saving only the child of the fellow black. She is also the little girl scalped and drowned whose lock of hair with red ribbon still attached floated in the Ohio river until found by Paul D (180). Killed both by the white "men with no skin" (214) and by the black mothers who in despair "went into the sea without smiling at me," or who in deadly grasp of their own "Precious thing" "whispered to me, chewed me, and swam away" (214), Beloved is aborted and outlawed, "disremembered and unaccounted for," reduced like the voices in the wind of Brooks's poem to "wind in the eaves. Just weather" (275).

*

But weather is what we live in. And the novel's last word, a naming, embracing "Beloved," contradicts the erasure that was enacted. It circles back to the novel's first word, a title projected from a biblical headnote proclaiming "I will call them my people, which were not my people, and her beloved, which was not beloved" (Rom. 9:1). These references testify to the truly audacious claim the mother in this novel, of this dis(re)membered child, makes. Not, as the community originally felt, that Sethe believed her right over her child's life was as the creator's, God's, the potter's right over the clay (Rom. 9:21). But rather that she believed in her right to her place in the grieving, remembering pietà *despite* her responsibility for that death.

In her headnote, Morrison invokes the epistle where Paul (not for nothing is the novel's male protagonist called Paul) describes the opening of the covenant, the widening of the blessing, from the narrow confines of the Jewish "law" of "righteousness" to the whole world of those who can pass, in faith, the "stumblingstone, the rock of offense" which is the dead Jesus, the dead child in the lap of the mother (Rom. 9:32–33). Paul notes the readiness of those born into a particular moral code to believe they need seek no further for the domain of spirit, and counsels a more mystic, less wordbound faith. Julia Kristeva, in a brilliant treatment of the pietà figure in "Stabat Mater," notes that the metaphors of maternal milk and tears, mystically conflated in the pietà's dead child at the mother's breast, so prominent in Morrison's novel, too, "are the metaphors of nonspeech, of a 'semiotics' that linguistic communication does not account for" but which nevertheless speaks of the integration of death and rebirth (174). "The Mother and her attributes," the milk that is the ink which enables the word, the body, of the child, and the tears which point to, which allow/accept, its death, are a potent prespeech, post-Logos, for Kristeva "a signifying disposition that is closer to so-called primary processes" (174) than verbalization. Morrison's Sethe made the ink that wrote the words that erased the humanity of her race and gender: she bore (made/suffered) the death that logically followed. She also carried the milk that, stolen, always replenished itself, and cried the tears a hungry world craved equally with her milk, tears of rage, grief, power, a "jouissance" not entirely subsumed by the maternal gaze upon the individual child, a "jouissance" ultimately, as Kristeva says of the Bellini paintings whose madonnas look away from the child towards an invisible place, not representable at all. Sethe, the infanticide, is in the fallen world. But also, breast to breast with the dead (made) being whom she has just handed on to "the other place," she is in "the other place," too, a figure of sublimity. Evoking these ancient figures, claiming these sacred sources, Morrison's boldly appropriated pietà is designed to stop all words but one, the first and last in its text.

Our culture, its languages of reason and argument a deafening roar of "mine"—my body, my baby, my mother, my meaning, my sin, my salvation—pauses, appalled, before the pietà, rock of offense, today most vividly (re)presented in the aborting woman. What word can allow us to pass it, if not, somehow equally distributed to the living figure and the dead one, "Beloved"?

Notes

Introduction

1. Julia Kristeva, "Stabat Mater," in *The Kristeva Reader*, ed. Toril Moi (New York: Columbia University Press, 1986), 161.

2. See, for instance, Dorothy Dinnerstein, *The Mermaid and the Minotaur: Sexual Arrangements and Human Malaise* (New York: Harper & Row, 1976), especially chapters 3 and 4; and Nancy Chodorow, *The Reproduction of Mothering: Psychoanalysis and the Sociology of Gender* (Los Angeles: University of California Press, 1978), especially chapters 5, 6, and 7.

3. Julia Kristeva, "Motherhood According to Giovanni Bellini," in *Desire in Language: A Semiotic Approach to Literary Art*, ed. Leon S. Roudiez (New York: Columbia University Press, 1980). Kristeva muses, "And yet . . . motherhood seems to be impelled *also* by a nonsymbolic, nonpaternal causality. . . . Material compulsion, spasm of a memory belonging to the species that either binds together or splits apart to perpetuate itself. . . . How can we verbalize this prelinguistic, unrepresentable memory? Heraclitus' flux, Epicurus' atoms, the whirling dust of cabalic, Arab and Indian mystics, and the stippled drawings of psychedelics—all seem better metaphors than the theories of Being, the logos, and its laws" (239). The essay goes on to distinguish the "jouissance" of this memory, located in the maternal subject, as captured eloquently in the madonna paintings of Bellini. Here, far from the depiction of a maternal gaze locked upon a fetishized child, the painter instead depicts the gaze of the mother fixed elsewhere, nowhere, summoning the viewer with herself to "the luminous serenity of the unrepresentable," the lost territory of original biopsychic memory (243).

4. E. Ann Kaplan, "Motherhood and Patriarchal Discourse," in *Women and Film* (New York: Methuen, Inc., 1983), 201.

5. Adrienne Rich, *Of Woman Born: Motherhood as Experience and Institution* (New York: W. W. Norton Co., 1976), 10.

6. Walker made this comment in an interview in 1973, printed later in her book of essays, *In Search of Our Mothers' Gardens* (New York: Harcourt, Brace, Jovanovich, 1983), 248.

7. Marsha Norman, *The Fortune Teller* (New York: Bantam Books, 1988), 310.

8. In a strongly polemical but wide-ranging and clearly argued essay in the pro-life *Human Life Review,* Eileen Farrell notes, accurately, that the testimony of literature, quantitatively at least, weighs in strongly against any *easy* choice of abortion. She proposes that "against the weight of this testimony, the most industrious campaign of 'true life stories' will have little to offer beyond the usual chaos" ("Abortion in Literature," *Human Life Review* 2 [Summer, 1985]: 79). Farrell's account seems to me to ignore the complexities of feminist protest in such novels as *Surfacing* and *Play It as It Lays.* And the "campaigns" of true life stories on both sides of the argument certainly have much to offer, if only the everlasting testimony of real life chaos as against the powerful ordering myths of the artists.

9. Kristin Luker, *Abortion and the Politics of Motherhood* (Berkeley, Calif.: University of California Press, 1984). See especially chapter 7.

10. The poem was originally published in the collection of the same name, 1973. Adrienne Rich, *Poems: Selected and New* (New York: W. W. Norton Co., 1975), 196–98.

11. Arnold quotes this newspaper report in "The Function of Criticism at the Present Time," 1865, in *Prose of the Victorian Period,* ed. William E. Buckler (Boston, Mass.: Houghton Mifflin Co., 1958), 432.

12. Lawrence Lader, *Abortion,* 1966 (Boston, Mass.: Beacon Press, 1967), 1.

13. Linda Bird Francke, *The Ambivalence of Abortion* (New York: Dell Publishing Co., 1978), 23.

14. Paula Ervin, *Women Exploited* (Huntingdon, Ind.: Our Sunday Visitor Press, 1985), 15.

15. Ellen Messer and Kathryn May, *Back Rooms: Voices from the Illegal Abortion Era* (New York: St. Martin's Press, 1988), xi.

16. I've chosen not to deal at length here with these studies. A place to start is *Men and Abortion: Lessons, Losses, and Love,* by Arthur B. Shostak and Gary McLough, with Lynn Seng (New York: Praeger Publishers, 1984). The authors worked with questionnaires returned by 1,000 men who had been through the abortion clinic process with their partners. The book includes profiles of individuals as well as statistical tables and long careful commentaries by the authors, both of whom have accompanied partners through abortion crises in which the decision was mutual. Of special interest, perhaps, are two chapters: one contrasting the moral dilemmas of a small and especially anguished group of male respondents who were deeply, morally opposed to abortion yet felt they needed to be with the partner who had made the decision, with those of "repeaters," men who had been "through" more than one abortion; and another chapter offering four very thoughtful essays by some of the men who have volunteered to be counsellors for men in abortion clinics or somewhere in the process.

17. Lawrence Lader describes the Aristotelian triple soul process, and

notes that Aristotle distinguished between the probable point of "animation" for a male soul (forty days) and a female soul (eighty to ninety days), in *Abortion*, 77.

18. The Hippocratic oath itself is a subject for contemporary quarreling among historians of medicine. Lawrence Lader argues that "the most accepted theory today is that the anti-abortion section was written into the oath by Hippocratic disciples—that small, austere Pythagorean sect which preached that the soul was infused into the body at the moment of conception" (*Abortion*, 76). Justice Blackmun was especially impressed by this argument, it appears, during Supreme Court deliberations over *Roe vs. Wade*. See Miriam Faux, *Roe vs. Wade: The Untold Story of the Landmark Supreme Court Decision* (New York: Macmillan Co., 1988), 289, 296–98.

19. Lawrence Lader's analyses of the ways in which the population needs of states have intertwined with the moral/social encouragement or discouragement of abortion and birth control policies are arresting. See especially 81–84, and chapters 14, "The Lessons from European Abortion," and 15, "The Lesson of Japan," in *Abortion*.

20. Herbert Packer, a lawyer on the faculty of Stanford University, and Ralph Gampell, a lawyer-physician specializing in forensic medicine, published the results of their study in the *Stanford Law Review*. The article provided the impetus for the first abortion reform bill in California. Herbert Packer and Ralph Gampell, "Therapeutic Abortion: A Problem in Law and Medicine," *Stanford Law Review* 11 (May 1989).

21. Diane Schulder and Florynce Kennedy, *Abortion Rap* (New York: McGraw-Hill Co., 1971), 3–4.

22. Michel Foucault, *The History of Sexuality* (vol. 1, 1976) (New York: Random House, 1978), 69.

23. Carol Gilligan, *In a Different Voice*, 1982 (Cambridge, Mass.: Harvard University Press, 1983). See especially 70–75.

24. Christian tradition often conflates the unnamed woman taken in adultery whom Jesus saves from stoning (John 8:7) and the unnamed female public sinner who bathed Jesus' feet with costly oil and was forgiven for "loving much" (Luke 7:47), with Mary Magdalen, who is the only person named by all four gospels as the discoverer of the empty tomb and the spreader of the "good news" of the Resurrection.

25. Tony Tanner, *Adultery in the Novel: Contract and Transgression* (Baltimore, Md.: The Johns Hopkins University Press, 1979), 17.

26. All Austen novels are quoted from the Modern Library edition of *The Complete Novels of Jane Austen* (New York: Random House, Inc., 1962), this scene is in *Persuasion*, 1258.

27. Emily Brontë, *Wuthering Heights*, Norton Critical Edition (New York: W. W. Norton Co., 1972), 107.

28. Samuel Richardson, *Clarissa,* 1748 (New York: Dutton Press, 1968), 4:101.

29. Thomas Hardy, *Tess of the D'Urbervilles,* 1891 (Boston, Mass.: Houghton-Mifflin Press, 1960), 87.

30. Leo Tolstoy, *Anna Karenina,* 1878; trans. Louise and Aulmer Maude (New York: W. W. Norton Co., 1970), 264.

31. Nathaniel Hawthorne, *The Scarlet Letter,* 1850 (New York: W. W. Norton Co., 1961), 140.

32. Mrs. Frances Trollope, *Jessie Phillips, A Tale of the New Poor Law* (London: Colburn, 1844).

33. Walter Scott, *The Heart of Midlothian,* 1818 (London: J. M. Dent & Sons Ltd., 1978), 246.

34. I have treated these matters, especially that of the failure of "sisterhood" between "the good" and "the bad" sister, at greater length in *Secret Leaves: The Novels of Walter Scott* (Chicago, Ill.: The University of Chicago Press, 1980), chapter, 4.

35. George Eliot, *Adam Bede,* 1859 (London: J. M. Dent & Sons Ltd., 1976), 435.

36. Virginia Woolf, *Between the Acts,* 1941 (New York: Harcourt, Brace, Jovanovich, 1969), 152.

37. The story of the Bourne trial is told in Lawrence Lader's *Abortion,* 103–6.

38. William Goldman, *Boys and Girls Together,* 1964 (New York: Bantam Books, 1965), 583.

39. John Updike, *Rabbit Is Rich,* 1981 (New York: Ballantine Books, 1982), 19.

40. Barbara Johnson, "Apostrophe, Animation, and Abortion," *Diacritics* 16 (Spring 1987): 34.

41. Norman Mailer, *The Prisoner of Sex* (New York: New American Library, 1971), 140.

42. Barbara Smith, "Toward a Black Feminist Criticism," in *The New Feminist Criticism,* ed. Elaine Showalter (New York: Pantheon Books, 1985), 170.

43. Barbara Christian, *Black Women Novelists: The Development of a Tradition, 1892–1976* (Westport, Conn.: Greenwood Press, 1980), 184.

Chapter One: Barth and Drabble

1. John Barth, *The End of the Road,* 1958 (New York: Grossett and Dunlap, 1969), 112.

2. No other critic, as far as I know, has suggested that Rennie's pregnancy might not be "real." Most feel that the pregnancy, and especially the abortion scene, call Barth's tragicomic novel uncomfortably away from its intellectual games and into the traditional mimesis which enforces feeling,

not just thinking, on the reader; that here "there is too much actuality for the farce," as David Kerner phrases it in his essay, "Psychodrama in Eden" (*Chicago Review,* Winter/Spring 1959; reprinted in *Critical Essays on John Barth,* ed. Joseph Waldmeir [Boston, Mass.: G. K. Hall & Co., 1980], 94). My reading makes Rennie a potential player, not just a passive quantum of being to be shaped by warring male God and Devil, not just a quantum of "body" doomed to the "ravages which all [that is merely] flesh is heir to." Charles B. Harris, *Passionate Virtuosity* (Urbana, Ill.: University of Illinois Press, 1983), 43.

3. John Barth, *Sabbatical,* 1982 (Harmondsworth, Middlesex: Penguin Books, Ltd., 1983), 53.

4. Flannery O'Connor, "A Good Man Is Hard to Find," in *Flannery O'Connor: The Complete Stories* (New York: Farrar, Straus & Giroux, 1972), 133.

5. John O. Stark describes the twins motif as emblematic of Barth's theme of opposites in *The Literature of Exhaustion* (Durham, N. C.: Duke University Press, 1974), 148–55.

6. E. P. Walkiewicz elaborates that the book's "biological conceit" is to follow two eggs traveling down the fallopian tubes toward an encounter with a spermatozoon. This "reminds us of . . . the power of the artist to fecundate the twin ova of fact and fancy within the protected microcosm of his fiction." E. P. Walkiewicz, *John Barth* (Boston, Mass.: Twayne Publishers, 1986), 144.

7. See Barth's "The Literature of Exhaustion," *Atlantic,* August 1967, 29–35.

8. Valerie Grosvenor Myer's *Margaret Drabble: Puritanism and Permissivism* (New York: Barnes & Noble, 1974) offered an account of this Calvinist fatality as essentially the object of a critique by Drabble. Mary Hurley Moran's *Margaret Drabble: Existing Within Structures* (Carbondale, Ill.: Southern Illinois University Press, 1983) argues still more cogently, I think, that Drabble's attitude towards the legacy of both Greek and Christian forms of fatalism has at once the quality of critical examination and of resignation, even irascible celebration, of this legacy. Moran quotes Drabble herself: "[My characters] seek identity, . . . but they do not seek freedom or liberation. These concepts have very little meaning for me. We are not free from our past, we are never free of the claims of others, and we ought not to wish to be." For Moran, the forces in the novels, "non-rational and atavistic," that partially direct the human being's formation of his/her "identity" beyond the grasp of his/her "will," are tempered by grace (a psychological and metaphysical reality for Drabble) and imagination (16–17, 19).

9. Margaret Drabble, *The Millstone,* 1965 (New York: New American Library, 1984), 80.

10. Margaret Drabble, *The Middle Ground,* 1980 (New York: Bantam Books, 1982), 206–7.

11. Critics disagree on the enigma of the ending: though the novel seems structured to bring about an enlightened "synthesis" of independence and loving social connection in the protagonists, Rosamond's final immersion in the mother-child dyad strikes many as a retreat from the structure. Ellen Cronan Rose even argues that the mother love which rejects all outside it, even the father's love of the child, is no love at all. Ellen Cronan Rose, *Equivocal Figures: The Novels of Margaret Drabble* (New York: Barnes & Noble, Inc., 1980), 20–23. This skeptical reading of Rosamond as an unreliable narrator, pursued most clearly to its limits perhaps by Susan Spitzer in "Fantasy and Femaleness in Margaret Drabble's *The Millstone,*" *Novel* 11 (Spring 1978): 227–46, links *The Millstone* even more directly with *The End of the Road,* both of them "lies posing as autobiography" (the phrase is from Harris, *Passionate Virtuosity,* 40).

12. This negative, even nihilistic close, so like the exhausted "terminal" that closes *The End of the Road,* makes a powerful conclusion, pregnancy/birth functioning in Drabble as pregnancy/abortion does in Barth, to cut off, or confirm the cutting off, of something. Lorna Irvine argues that the child in *The Millstone* is one of the correlatives for the commitment to "continuance," the awarding of a future to her characters, that marks all Drabble's works. Lorna Irvine, "No Sense of an Ending: Drabble's Continuous Fictions," in *Critical Essays on Margaret Drabble,* ed. Ellen Cronan Rose (Boston, Mass.: G. K. Hall & Co., 1985), 76. My own reading is that birth functions much less directly in that way here, paradoxically enough, than does abortion in *The Middle Ground.*

13. This refusal to "sum up," or rather, this tendency to sum up again and again and then dissolve the sums into a rich or bewildered multiplicity of possible judgments on, or directions for, her characters, is typical of Drabble's novels, a quality not all critics like as well as I do. Lynn V. Sadler calls it part of a "developing archness" in Drabble's most recent novels, beginning especially with *The Middle Ground.* Lynn V. Sadler, *Margaret Drabble* (Boston, Mass.: G. K. Hall & Co., 1986), 119.

Chapter Two: Didion, Atwood, Gordon, Piercy

1. Marge Piercy, *Braided Lives,* 1982 (New York: Ballantine Books, 1982), 212.

2. Joan Didion, *Play It as It Lays,* 1970 (New York: Bantam Books, 1971), 48.

3. Mary Gordon, *The Company of Women,* 1980 (New York: Ballantine Books, 1982), 267–68.

4. P. 10. Cynthia Griffin Woolf, noting Maria's emphatic levering up of the middle syllable of her name—"That is pronounced Mar-*eye*-ah, to get it

straight at the outset" (2)—argues that Didion's heroine thus draws attention to her gallantly doomed attempt to wrest "the gaze" away from the men in the novel who absolutely own it, to be the eye that simply sees, instead of the male eye that cuts, places, arranges. Cynthia Griffin Woolf, "Didion and the New American Heroine," in *Joan Didion: Essays and Conversations*, ed. Ellen G. Friedman (Princeton, N.J.: Ontario Review Press, 1984), 129–30.

5. Critic Judi Roller notes that in one kind of feminist novel, exemplified especially by Doris Lessing's *The Golden Notebook*, the child is precisely "that which, without question, one must stay sane for." Judi Roller, *The Politics of the Feminist Novel* (New York: Greenwood Press, 1986), 166. At the same time another kind exists where the child is, at least partially, a negative symbol, a tradition perhaps most memorably, if confusingly, expressed by Edna Pontellier's affirmation, in Kate Chopin's *The Awakening*, that while she would die for her children, she will not live for them. This stance is more complexly dramatized, as we shall see, in Marge Piercy's careful distinction between the child as an emblem of the desire of the fathers to possess women, and the child as, equally with all humans, an object of care.

6. Barry Chabot, for one, sees no self-rescue or child-rescue at the novel's end, only Maria's continuing complicity in her own anesthetization, self-abortion: "The 'nothing' Maria takes some pride in having faced is . . . her haven as well as her grief." Barry Chabot, "Joan Didion's *Play It as It Lays* and the Vacuity of the 'Here and Now'," in *Joan Didion: Essays and Conversations*. Mark Royden Winchell agrees: "No, Maria is not Prince Hamlet, nor was she meant to be. What we have in *Play It as It Lays* is a kind of post-existential nihilism which . . . obviates the necessity of passing judgement . . . on anything at all." Mark Royden Winchell, *Joan Didion* (Boston, Mass.: Twayne Publishers, 1980), 137.

7. Margaret Atwood, *Surfacing*, 1972 (New York: Popular Books, 1976), 168.

8. Marilyn Yalom, like other critics, has linked Atwood's novel with Sylvia Plath's *The Bell Jar* through this image of the bottle, evocative of the "protection" that kills, the preserving that mocks life. Plath's Esther, like Atwood's narrator, has recoiled from the terrors of birth and birthing—"Here was a woman in terrible pain, obviously feeling every bit of it . . . and she would go straight home and start another baby, because the drug would make her forget how bad the pain had been, when all the time, in some secret part of her, that long, blind, doorless and windowless corridor of pain was waiting to open up and shut her in again"—to the mad haven of the bell jar— "To the person in the bell jar, blank and stopped as a dead baby, the world itself is the bad dream." Sylvia Plath, *The Bell Jar*, 1963 (New York: Bantam Books, 1972), 53, 193. Yalom also sees the recuperation of the jar image through the placement of the saving/saved and sacred

baby inside a transparent womb or maternal belly. Marilyn Yalom, *Maternity, Mortality and the Literature of Madness* (University Park, Pa.: Pennsylvania State University Press, 1985), 88.

9. Barbara Hill Rigney in *Madness and Sexual Politics in the Feminist Novel* (Madison, Wis.: University of Wisconsin Press, 1978) connects the enforced abortion with a deeper split, the psychological suicide the narrator has accepted as signified by a progressive cutting off, head from body, thumb from hand (97). Thus the abortion is an effect, not a cause. This fragmentation has masqueraded as unity. "The specious unity offered to women by man-made feminine roles" is a particular target of the feminist novel of madness, argues Marilyn Yalom (*Maternity, Mortality and the Literature of Madness*, 67).

10. In somewhat "masculinist" language, the *Atlantic*'s reviewer, Benjamin DeMott, contemplates this "fall": "Keen, enthusiastic, self-centered, condescending to her elders . . . Felicitas Taylor has to be brought down, and at length she is. . . . She finds herself pregnant." *Atlantic*, March 1981, 89. Writing in the *New York Times Book Review* (15 February 1981, 24) Francine du Plessix Gray notes the final refusal of the book to abandon "singularity" as a value for females as well as males, calling it a "fascinating streak of Monastic Amazonism."

11. The unanimity with which early reviewers reject Robert Cavendish and the whole central 1960s section of the novel as "unrealistic" and "unconvincing" is striking. Both du Plessix Gray, ibid., and Barbara Grizzutti Harrison, for instance, found the priest believable, even "finely rendered," but the professor and the Columbia episode false: "We've heard it all before and we have trouble believing Felicitas would fall in love with this mean and stupid professor." Grizzutti Harrison, *Saturday Review*, February 1981, 63. If we have experience of these things, of course we have no trouble believing they happen. Gordon's most significant move here is to award Father Cyprian a final monologue which clarifies both the pathos and the sincerity of his inner life, renders his verdict upon himself as a fourth dimension of his psyche. What we know of Robert's inner life we deduce from his less guarded moments at mid-book, and perhaps from pondering his similarity with Cyprian. To decline to do such deducing is to settle for the same old sixties bashing, though it is true, too, that Gordon's refusal to return to Robert's mind in the final monologues diminishes him.

12. *Excess* is the word reviewers most often used for Piercy's novel, an excess found not so much in the style but in the many events of the plot. Things happen relentlessly, daily, monthly, in the novel, even conspiratorily, as they do (or seem to the harassed female psyche to do) in the female body. Katha Pollitt, in an otherwise hospitable account in the *New York Times Book Review*, 7 February 1982, 7, "wishes she had let a part stand for the whole" instead of visiting the whole catalogue of social cruelties and

treacheries upon her characters. But Piercy is not satisfied to *represent*, she wants to *demonstrate*, with that particularity and repetition which will always involve artistic excess, the fate of the resisting female psyche in a very physical, as well as patriarchal, universe.

Chapter Three: Hemingway, Faulkner, Keneally, Swift, Irving

1. William Faulkner, *As I Lay Dying*, 1930 (New York: Random House, Inc., 1957), 164.

2. Quotations from Ernest Hemingway's short stories "Indian Camp" (first published 1925) and "Hills Like White Elephants" (first published 1927) are from the collection, *The Short Stories of Ernest Hemingway* (New York: Charles Scribner's Sons, 1938). This quotation is from 94.

3. Thomas Keneally, *Passenger*, 1979 (Glasgow: Fontana Books; William Collins Son & Co. Ltd., 1980), 47.

4. Graham Swift, *Waterland*, 1983 (New York: Washington Square Press, 1985), 13.

5. John Irving, *The Cider House Rules*, 1985 (New York: Bantam Books, 1986), 567.

6. Marilyn Yalom (*Maternity, Mortality and Madness*) links war and childbirth as triggering agencies, in works of literature, for madness, clinically, or cycles of disintegration and re-integration, metaphorically (see chapter 7). They are "boundary situations" which force the male or female psyche, respectively, past its ordinary social limits and into the domain of the heroic.

7. Faulkner criticism locates the title's source in the eleventh book of *The Odyssey*. Encountered in hell, Agamemnon reports bitterly to the questing Ulysses that his murdering wife refused him the last services: "As I lay dying, the woman with the dog's eyes would not close my eyelids for me as I descended into Hades." This inclines many to follow the novel as a male journey, Anse's or Darl's. Faulkner's appropriation of the words for his (dead) female protagonist, on the other hand, allows Mimi Gladstein to concentrate on the journey as a restaging of the Demeter and Persephone myth: Addie, the mother, journeying to the underworld to release the daughter, Dewey Dell. Mimi Gladstein, "Mother and Daughter in Endless Procession," in *Faulkner and Women*, ed. Doreen Fowler and A. J. Abadie (Jackson, Miss.: University Press of Mississippi, 1985), 106. The journey is ironic, of course; this Demeter cannot release herself or her daughter from the dire fertility imposed by the novel's world.

8. John N. Duvall notes the tendency of critics to reflect their own social desires in taking positions on Faulkner's women. This is especially the case when critics deal with this novel's Addie and Dewey Dell, and *The Wild Palms*'s Charlotte, women who seek a way out of the maternal sainthood pressed on them by a yearning culture, and by such Faulknerian foremothers as *Light in August*'s Lena Grove. John N. Duvall, "Faulkner's Critics and Wom-

en: The Voice of the Community," in *Faulkner and Women*, 43–44). The early work of Sally Page (*Faulkner's Women: Characterization and Meaning* [DeLand, Fla.: Everett/Edwards, 1972]) set up this image of the maternal goddess as characteristic of Faulkner's worldview, and the later, more cautious analysis of David Williams in *Faulkner's Women: The Myth and the Muse* (Montreal: McGill-Queens University Press, 1977) continues it. Williams's book complexifies the figure of the Faulknerian "awesome mother" by noting that the "Sacred Grove," the "Great Round," which the mythic mother rules in pre-Christian texts and which the male can be a part of "only as a child," is a scene of sacrifice, terror, and blood, as well as of beauty and fertility (see especially 105–10).

9. Addie herself "describes freedom of consciousness in terms of emptying out," notes James A. Snead in a recent adventurous and compelling book; she "recaptures a sense of the real through double negation." James A. Snead, *Figures of Division: William Faulkner's Major Novels* (New York: Methuen Press, 1986), 48, 68.

10. Reviewers generally admired Keneally's audacious and highly "crafted" fable, Clara Claiborne Park noting that, "on a subject that invites it, Keneally does not even graze sentimentality." Clara Claiborne Park, *Hudson Review* 32 (Winter 1979–80): 573. Another noted of this same "ungrazed" subject that the novel "carries powerful moral implications about abortion" without overtly preaching them. Edmund Fuller, *Sewanee Review* 88 (January 1980): iv. It is interesting to compare these with the reviews of John Irving's *The Cider House Rules*, by and large hostile, which saw Irving's more "Victorian" novel as inclining to the sentimental and the preachy. Keneally's stylistic animation of the fetus, of course, cleverly allows him to practice the pro-life stance without preaching it.

11. F. Scott Fitzgerald, *Tender Is the Night*, 1933 (New York: Charles Scribner's Sons, 1962), 57.

12. Reviewers, attracted to the ironic and Joycean excess of *Waterland* yet wary of it, tended only occasionally to catch the psycho-historical parallel between the myth of progress and the myth of control exercised by the patriarchy, a connection hidden by Swift's decision to situate the patriarchs on the maternal side of Tom Crick's family tree. It is probably true to say, however, that the antipatriarchal and conservationist counter-reality valued in the book is not "feminist," that is, water loving, but rather, as one reviewer put it, the conservatism of the classical stoic. See Michael Gorra, *The Nation*, 31 March 1984, 392.

13. Carol C. Harter and James R. Thompson share with many other readers a curious conviction that Irving has failed in this novel to dramatize "the undertoad," that principle of "radical disorder . . . terrifying contingency," which drives the "powerful engine" of his plots, and that this drains the novel of the "great *energy*," which usually comes in Irving novels

from the collision of the moral mind with this principle. Carol C. Harter and James R. Thompson, *John Irving* (Boston, Mass.: G. K. Hall & Co., 1986), 143. Here is where I believe he dramatizes it. They also share with other readers and critics the sense that Irving has not provided sufficient "polarity" between Dr. Larch's pro-choice stance and the purely pro-life stance. See, for instance, David Montrose's review in the *Times Literary Supplement*, 21 June 1985, 689: "Irving is not, of course, obliged to present both sides of the question, but his failure to do so passes up an opportunity for productive conflict." Larch's protégé, Homer, suffers this productive conflict in half a dozen scenes throughout the novel; the fact that he ultimately and reluctantly takes the pro-choice position in the end seems to have weighed more strongly in these readers' minds than the facts of the conflict.

Chapter Four: Walker, Hansberry, Naylor, Jones, Williams, Morrison

1. Herbert G. Gutman, *The Black Family in Slavery and Freedom, 1750– 1925* (New York: Vintage Books, 1976), 75.

2. Gayle Jones, *Corregidora*, 1975 (Boston, Mass.: Beacon Press, 1986), 14, 10.

3. Toni Morrison, *The Bluest Eye*, 1970 (New York: Washington Square Press, 1972), 148.

4. Ntzake Shange, *For Colored Girls Who Have Considered Suicide When the Rainbow Is Enuf* (New York: Macmillan Co., 1978), 22.

5. Alice Walker, *Meridian*, 1976 (New York: Washington Square Press, 1977), 114–15.

6. The interview was later published in Walker's *In Search of Our Mothers' Gardens*. This story is on 246–47.

7. Walker's comment is contained in a letter she wrote to the editors of the *Black Scholar*, published in *In Search of Our Mothers' Gardens*, 324. She had considerable praise for Wallace's exposé of the sexism and ignorance in black male attitudes towards black women (323) but took issue with the book's suggestion that no black women writers had challenged the male stereotypes of the black matriarch before.

8. *A Street in Bronzeville* was later published as part of *The World of Gwendolyn Brooks* (New York: Harper and Row, 1971); "kitchenette building" appears on 5, "the mother" appears on 5–6. Hazel Carby makes the interesting comment that in the attempt to establish a clear and coherent tradition of black women's writing, an emphasis has been laid on a "rural" tradition running back to Zora Neale Hurston, an emphasis that has, in some minds at least, "marginalized" the important tradition of urban writing focused on "the street." Hazel Carby, *Reconstructing Womanhood: The Emergence of the Afro-American Woman Novelist* (New York: Oxford University Press, 1987), 173. Brooks's 1945 book of poems is central to this

tradition, as is Ann Petry's 1946 novel *The Street,* where a young black woman with a deserting husband and an eight-year-old son struggles to move up from the grime and crime of Harlem's 116th Street, only to be blocked at every turn by the white (actually "gray") man who controls the street's racial, financial, and even sexual economies (Reprint, Boston, Mass.: Beacon Press, 1985).

9. Hughes's "Harlem" was first published in *Montage on a Dream Deferred* (New York: Henry Holt, 1951), 71.

10. Lorraine Hansberry, *A Raisin in the Sun* (first published, and produced on Broadway, 1959) (New York: New American Library, 1966), 34, 33.

11. The black matriarch, this "epic figure who entered [my] consciousness as a child," came to Hansberry at least as much through the poetry of Langston Hughes as through familial experience, notes Ann Cheney in *Lorraine Hansberry* (Boston, Mass.: G. K. Hall Inc., 1984), 65. Cheney suggests that the relationship between Mama and Walter Lee, the grown man still a "project" of his mother, echoes the relationship in Hughes's poem "Mother to Son." In an important essay in *Freedomways* Adrienne Rich describes the "problem and the challenge" of Hansberry's play, which gives the central dramaturgical and radicalizing changes to the male son. Was it strategy, or self-censorship, Rich wonders, that made the same woman who praised the much maligned black matriarch for being the one who refused to move to the back of the bus in Montgomery construct a play in which the matriarch works for radicalization through her son? Adrienne Rich, "The Problem with Lorraine Hansberry," *Freedomways* 19, no. 4 (1979): 247–55.

12. Gloria Naylor, *The Women of Brewster Place,* 1982 (New York: Penguin Books, 1983), 25.

13. The reviewer in the *New Republic* claims that there is no "wariness" in the novel about motherhood, that the concept of motherhood is "embraced by Naylor's women, each of whom is a surrogate child or mother to the next." Dorothy Wickenden, *New Republic,* 6 September 1982, 37. This is true of those I've just discussed, though the book is clearly troubled by the pressure imposed on some to be forever mothers, the helpless license taken by others to be forever children. The novel complexifies this still further in its final story, in which a lesbian couple is ostracized by all the surrogate mothers of the community. In the novel's dark climax, Lorraine, the more fragile lesbian partner, is gang raped because she is simultaneously the representative of the women and the one cast out even by them, "a blood sacrifice brutally proving the sisterhood of all women" as Annie Gottlieb put it in the *New York Times Book Review,* 22 August 1982, 25.

14. Marsha Darling, "In the Realm of Responsibility: A Conversation with Toni Morrison," *The Women's Review of Books,* March 1988, 5–6.

15. Michael Awkward has argued persuasively that the rape episode in *The Bluest Eye* is a "refiguration" of the Trueblood episode in Ralph Ellison's *Invisible Man,* one which "authenticates specific types of black and feminine experience whose value and significance [the Ellison text] by overt and covert means—denies." Michael Awkward, "Roadblocks and Relatives: Critical Revision in Toni Morrison's *The Bluest Eye,"* in *Critical Essays on Toni Morrison,* ed. Nellie Y. McKay (Boston, Mass.: G. K. Hall & Co., 1988), 58. In Ellison's book a black father who raped his daughter is a subject of awe and terror to the white men of the neighborhood, but no report is made on the daughter's experience or her pregnancy. In Morrison's novel the child-observer Claudia MacTeer notes that her neighborhood was scandalized and titilated: "They were disgusted, amused, shocked, outraged or even excited by the story. But we listened for the ones who would say, 'poor little girl,' or 'poor baby,' but there was only head wagging where those words should have been. We looked for eyes creased with concern, but saw only veils" (148).

16. This domain, which I've called the mystified present, is eloquently described in another kind of time line by Barbara Christian as an equally mystified spring, with its "circular structure, its ironically rhythmical patterns, its theme of inversion in which old men are inverted Daddies struggling for a meaning in life by touching the first twigs of spring." "In arranging such a pattern," Christian continues, "Morrison has wrested out of the March winds . . . her characters' desire to be reborn, even if tragic forms are their only fruit" (*Black Women Novelists,* 150).

17. Toni Cade Bambara, *The Salt Eaters,* 1980 (New York: Vintage Books, 1981), 295.

18. Sherley Anne Williams, *Dessa Rose,* 1986 (New York: Berkley Books, 1987), 198.

19. Toni Morrison, *Beloved* (New York: Alfred A. Knopf, 1987), 273.

20. Kristeva, "Stabat Mater," 162.

21. Valerie Smith, *Self-Discovery and Authority in Afro-American Narrative* (Cambridge, Mass.: Harvard University Press). See introduction, 1–5.

Index

Index